# Selling to Uncle Sam

# Selling to Uncle Sam

## How to Win Choice Government Contracts for Your Business


Clinton L. Crownover

Mark Henricks





McGraw-Hill, Inc.

New York San Francisco Washington, D.C. Auckland Bogotá
Caracas Lisbon London Madrid Mexico City Milan
Montreal New Delhi San Juan Singapore
Sydney Tokyo Toronto

**Library of Congress Cataloging-in-Publication Data**

Crownover, Clinton L.
Selling to Uncle Sam : how to win choice government contracts for your business / Clinton L. Crownover, Mark Henricks.
p. cm.
Includes index.
ISBN 0-07-014834-1 — ISBN 0-07-014851-1 (pbk.)
1. Public contracts—United States. 2. Contracts, Letting of —United States. 3. Government purchasing—United States. 4. Marketing—United States. I. Henricks, Mark. II. Title.
HD3861.U6C76 1993
658.8'04—dc20 93-38
CIP



1 2 3 4 5 6 7 8 9 0 DOC/DOC 9 9 8 7 6 5 4 3

ISBN 0-07-014834-1 {HARD}
ISBN 0-07-014851-1 {SOFT}

*The sponsoring editor for this book was Caroline Carney, the editing supervisor was Frances Koblin, and the production supervisor was Donald Schmidt. It was set in Palatino by McGraw-Hill's Professional Book Group composition unit.*

*Printed and bound by R. R. Donnelley & Sons Company*

DISCLAIMER

This book contains the author's opinion on the subject. Neither the author nor the publisher is engaged in offering legal, tax, accounting, investment, or similar professional services. Some material may be affected by changes in the law or in the interpretation of laws since the book was written. Laws also vary from state to state. Therefore, no guarantee can be given as to the accuracy and completeness of information. In adddition, recommendations made by the author as well as strategies outlined in the text may not necessarily be suitable depending on changes or new interpretations of the law or depending upon a reader's personal financial situation. For legal, tax, accounting, investment, or other professional advice, it is suggested that the reader consult a competent practitioner. The author hereby specifically disclaims any liability for loss incurred as a consequence of any material presented in this book.

This book is printed on recycled, acid-free paper containing a minimum of 50% recycled de-inked fiber.

# Contents

# Preface

Corporate scale-downs have resulted in a new age of assessment. Each of us, whether we like it or not, is going to have to look at ways of becoming leaner and meaner. The federal government, the largest business in the world, has initiated major cutbacks in procurement of goods and services. In addition to these cutbacks the government has instituted regulations that sharpen the edge on the knife that slices the pie.

Competition in federal procurement is stiffer, stronger, and keener than it has ever been. A massive amount of time is required to research, understand, and formulate a bid for Uncle Sam. Skill and expertise are needed in knowing how to present your talents and capabilities in a manner that will win you business. You must ascertain what it is you are being required to do and the implications of providing that good or service. It is with this objective that *Selling to Uncle Sam* has been written.

In order to succeed in government contracting, you have to know your company and know the government's needs and how to fulfill them.

The first requirement, knowing your company, we leave largely up to you, aside from explaining a few ways in which you can assess your company's ability to meet the government's needs and maximize your company's perceived value in the eyes of government contracting officials.

The second requirement, learning what the government needs and how to provide it, is our province. In *Selling to Uncle Sam* you will find one of the first full explanations of how to understand and fill the government's needs. It guides you from your early tentative steps of exploration, through all the inevitable red tape, down to the final negotiation and eventual contract award.

This is not a book of lists directing you to the pot of gold at the end of the rainbow. It is a step-by-step instructional reference that will help you approach the field of government procurement, whether it be for the first time, or for the ten thousandth time. It brings you information and experience from the point of view of a small business owner. The information provided in the following pages is designed to give you an edge on your competition and help you keep that edge. Whether you are a business owner, a program manager, or a part of the bid and proposal effort, you will find something in this book that will help you in your daily responsibilities.

There is yet another reason for this book—change. The government may look monolithic and unchanging from here, but the fact is, it is always in the middle of one or more dramatic shifts. You can keep up with many of the changes in government buying by reading periodicals, attending seminars, and simply immersing yourself in the flow of government business. But from time to time, as practices change in both general and government business, it takes a new book on the subject to wrap it all up in an up-to-date, comprehensive package.

The most critical change of the last couple of years for the government contractor—and for a lot of other people besides—is the end of the Cold War era. What that means for the world has yet to be completely shaken out, but for the government contractor it means that defense contracting opportunities will never be the same as they were in the post-World War II era.

And there is yet another kind of change that calls for this book. As big as the U.S. government is, it doesn't operate in a vacuum, either. Government contracting has not remained isolated from a sweeping shift in business practices in the private sector. If you've been intrigued about the possibilities for improvement contained in the latest trends in management, from total quality to benchmarking, so have government buyers. This book, written in the midst of the bubbling environment of 1990s-style business innovation and tempered with years of government contracting experience, brings those two worlds together just as you will experience them in your daily practice.

We think the ideas, approaches, and techniques offered in *Selling to Uncle Sam* represent a different approach to selling to the government, one that emphasizes the business aspects and brings government contracting practices up to date at a particularly important time for the private and public sectors. For those who run small businesses, every minute and every sale are important. This book is intended to save you time, effort, and money by guiding your way so you don't have to rely on costly consultants or time-wasting trial and error. We are confident that as a result of reading this book and implementing its recommendations, you will be better prepared to get out there and do the thing that's best for the government and for you, namely, make the sale.

And last, we would like to acknowledge those who provided their support and input for this book. To our wives, Teresa and Barbara, and the children, Matthew and Jason, thanks for being patient. To our friends and business associates, your time and input are deeply appreciated.

*Clinton L. Crownover*
*Mark Henricks*

# Selling to Uncle Sam

# 1

# Biggest Market, Toughest Rules, Sweetest Payoff

## An Opportunity of, by, and for Everyone

Uncle Sam buys more of everything than anybody in the world. That's a big statement, but it's easy to believe when you take a look at the volume and variety of government purchases.

### A Big Slice of Pie

Each year over $210 billion flows out of Washington, D.C., and into businesses large and small. The U.S. government's annual spending spree dwarfs outlays by any other national government, not to mention mere private corporations.

About 20 percent of federal government procurement outlays winds up going to small businesses of various kinds, according to the Small Business Administration (SBA). And, says Gene VanArsdale, director of the SBA's office of procurement policy and liaison, "The trend of small business share is very slightly upward. It's been bouncing around 19 percent for a while."

That's not a bad slice of pie, but it doesn't seem to attract as many small businesses competitors as you might think. Even the government doesn't claim to know exactly how many small businesses sell to it, but by one measure the number is a small minority of the nation's estimated 20 million small businesses. That measure consists of the roughly 210,000 firms listed in a computerized directory of small companies seeking deals with the federal government or its prime contractors.

Again, there's no data to show that small businesses are more or less likely to try to sell to the government today than yesterday. But one thing's sure. No matter what you think about the direction of future spending on defense, welfare entitlements, health care, Social Security or any other line item on the federal budget, it's a pretty safe bet that overall expenditures are going to continue going in one direction—up. That alone is reason enough to consider doing business with the government.

## An Omnivorous Appetite

Size isn't the only thing that makes the government market attractive. Uncle Sam is also the most omnivorous shopper on the planet. Anything used by consumers in the private sector is also used and purchased by the U.S. government—and then some.

In fact, some agency of the government quite likely *is* buying your product or service, or something like it, right now. All you have to do is figure out who it is and mount an effective government marketing campaign, and you can make the sale.

Once you have established yourself as a qualified supplier and positioned yourself on the mailing lists with the various government buyers, you may find yourself overwhelmed with the amount of solicitations you receive in the mail for review.

If the government does not currently buy your product, it may be they are just unaware of it. Unsolicited proposals are sent to the government daily by businesses such as yours that have come up with a better mousetrap. These unsolicited proposals are an avenue for introducing your good or service and may quite possibly lead to a lucrative contract if the government has a need.

## Selling with a Difference

Government marketing is not like marketing to the private sector. The expense-account lunches, the glad-handing patter, the polished sales presentations that characterize many sales efforts in other business arenas—all these are conspicuously absent from government marketing. If you have always relied on traditional sales techniques to generate business for your company, you are going to have to learn a new approach in order to sell to the government.

Learning a new way is not all bad. Reference Software International Inc., an $18 million maker of grammar-checking programs for personal computers, got into government marketing specifically because it wasn't like regular markets.

"We looked for a marketplace that had a clear distribution channel, a way of getting our products in front of as many people as possible without having a large sales staff," says Jeff Mallett, vice president of marketing and sales for the San Francisco company.

After a couple of years of plying government markets, using many of the same techniques described in this book, Reference Software was doing a profitable business with Washington worth $1 million a year.

Selling to the government isn't, however, a sure way to get rich. Those stories of $600 toilet seats and $3000 hammers are repeated for one reason: They're not the norm. For the most part, government marketing is for rigorous business people who pay close attention to costs, keep tight controls, are willing to discipline themselves to following government rules and regulations, and are in for the long haul.

But even that isn't enough. To sell to Uncle Sam, you have to be a good business person, and more. You must grasp the special tricks and techniques of government marketing. Once you learn those, there are plenty of good reasons why selling to Uncle Sam is an opportunity of, by, and for everyone.

## World's Biggest Market

What do you sell? Abrasives? Zinc ribbon? These products and virtually everything in between are all bought by Uncle Sam.

What about services? Are you an architectural firm? A tree-planting company? Do you officiate youth volleyball games? There is a place for you, and countless other service providers, in the world of government contracting.

For Biotechnical Services Inc., a 24-employee North Little Rock, Arkansas, company, even such an exotic service as toxicology research found buyers aplenty in the various agencies of the federal government. After six years working in the private sector and subcontracting to other government contractors, the first government contract President Judith McDowall landed was the company's biggest deal ever.

In one fell swoop, government business accounted for nearly half of Biotechnical Services' billings. "They do buy lots of work," confirms McDowall. "They're a big customer."

All told, the government is a regular customer for several million products and services. With that kind of variety, it's impossible to concisely and precisely characterize the amount and kinds of things the government purchases.

But let's look at just the areas of computers and telecommunications. Robert Dornan, vice president of market research for Federal Sources Inc., a McLean, Virginia, consultant to government contractors in those fields, said the government in fiscal year 1992 was budgeted to spend $17.6 billion on outside procurements of computers and telecommunications products and services.

"And that only covers general-purpose computers and telecommunications," adds Dornan. "It does not include some fairly exotic militarized computers and other things."

Going into more detail, the government's budget sets aside $4.2 billion for hardware purchase and lease, $4 billion for operations and maintenance services, and $2.8 billion for analysis and programming.

Sound like a lot? These are just the amounts for prime contracts. "The amount they take in subcontracts is almost impossible to compute but it's also substantial," says Dornan.

And that's only computers and telecommunications. Any attempt at a comprehensive description of all government purchases would take up many pages and inevitably leave many things out. And, because the government's needs constantly change, so do the things it buys. For instance, asbestos removal became a big business for government contractors after researchers determined the common fireproofing material was a health hazard. Today, in the wake of the massive savings and loan defaults, property management services are in demand at those government agencies that wound up as owners of vast amounts of foreclosed real estate.

Some things don't change, though. And, in general, you can break government-purchased products and services into two major groups: civilian and military. Many products such as, say, mattresses, are purchased by both the military and civilian wings of government. But other purchases are unique to or at least most likely to be bought by one or the other.

## Military Purchases

The Army, Navy, Air Force, Marines, and Coast Guard are the top military purchasing agencies. The U.S. Army Corps of Engineers, Defense

Logistics Agency, and Surgeon General are other major defense-related buyers.

What do they buy? Obviously, the military is the only buyer of things such as nuclear warheads and underwater mines. However, the military also consumes lots of products that aren't strictly connected with national defense. Examples include ready-mixed concrete, forklifts and vegetable-peeling machines.

The same is true of services. The military may be your only likely market if you are an expert at setting up computerized simulations of air combat. But the military also buys lots of nonmilitary services such as landscaping, well-drilling, painting, and more.

### Civilian Purchases

You can cover most of the military waterfront by listing just a few huge procuring agencies. But the civilian sector has many more purchasing agencies than does the military. In addition to such well-known agencies as the Federal Aviation Administration and the Social Security Administration, there are many less-recognized but no less valuable government buying opportunities at places like the U.S. Merchant Marine Academy and the Bureau of Prisons.

You may not realize that many well-known organizations are part of the federal government and, therefore, subject to the same rules as other government entities. Examples include the Tennessee Valley Authority, the National Guard, and the National Institutes of Health along with many lesser-known research centers around the country.

The civilian offices also purchase a wider variety of products and services than the military. You might find little interest in military buying circles for a shipment of animal feed, for instance. But the U.S. Department of Agriculture could snap up any number of carloads.

Likewise, if you sell lunar landing systems, NASA, a civilian agency, is your only real option, at least until the Air Force goes interplanetary.

### Some Restrictions

If the U.S. government market is the biggest and broadest in the world, it's still not without its limitations. There are a few categories of products and services that the government tries, with varying success, to buy from only certain sellers.

For instance, all U.S. agencies, military and civilian, are required to purchase household furniture from one of two sources: Federal Prison

Industries, an operation that employs inmates of federal penitentiaries, or companies that employ blind laborers. And there are quite a few other categories of products that carry the same stipulation, including gloves, pallets, metal signs, tarpaulins, trash cans, filing cabinets, and paint brushes.

This is not to say that there is no way you can ever sell any paint brushes or filing cabinets to an agency of the federal government. Not all these products are available all the time or in the right configuration to suit the needs of the federal buyers. When that happens, Uncle Sam reaches out to the open market, meaning you.

Some similar restrictions could limit your opportunity to sell some kinds of services to the government. For instance, printing and binding services. The U.S. government, through its Government Printing Office (GPO), is the world's largest printer and binder of books, pamphlets, manuals, and other printed matter. Government procurement offices are not allowed to purchase outside printing and binding services except on a waiver from the Government Printing Office.

The fact of the matter is, however, government agencies need more printing than even the GPO's enormous capacity can satisfy. Frequently, it gets behind and can't service rush or otherwise unusual orders. So your regional GPO office is a good place to look for printing work.

Another kind of restriction, one that you will like better, is a program called Small Business Set Aside. This program, along with a similar one encouraging government buyers to do business with minority-owned companies, is a restriction that is very beneficial to small companies. Both programs will be covered in detail in Chapter 2.

It should be emphasized that these two restrictions are not taken lightly by government contracting agencies. "They very effectively enforce that," consultant Dornan says, "so there is a huge amount of subcontract work farmed out to the small business community."

One more limitation that is invoked on some contracts ought to be dear to the heart of any small business that has been battered by foreign competition. For various reasons, mostly relating to national security, the government may decide that only domestic companies will be allowed to bid on and win a contract.

That means no undercutting by rivals in low-cost labor countries or unfair competition from countries that subsidize their own industries. This restriction has its limits, too, however. Even if you're up for one of these awards, you'll still have to compete against Canadian firms. There is also the possibility that neither you nor your competition is prohibited from buying parts from a low-cost labor country. But at least all competitors will have that opportunity.

A few limitations aside, as a general rule, the U.S. government market is, besides the biggest and broadest on the globe, the most open to competition. And some of the toughest rules anywhere keep it that way.

## Toughest Rules

Perhaps more so than in any other type of market, the government market is a world where rewards are based on merit. Popularity, charm, friendship—these attributes, valuable as they are in other walks of life, won't do you much good if in the end your bid for government business does not succeed on its own merits.

In government contracting, the race goes not necessarily to the swift or the beautiful, but to the steady and strong—and, of course, the low bidder.

### Low Bids

If your study of the government market has been spotty in recent years, or you've focused only on the headlines about influence peddling and overcharging, you may be of the opinion that there is little benefit in trying to be the low bidder on a government contract. Not so.

It's true that the low bidder does not *always* win the contract. But for most common government contracting opportunities, price is the overriding concern, assuming that you meet the basic requirements of the contract.

In other cases, the technical merit of your proposal may be as important as the price. These contracts often are for research and development of advanced technology, such as a new fighter plane or a data processing system, where companies are competing to offer the government the best design, and although cost must be competitive, it is a secondary concern.

Odds are, you won't be trying to sell the Air Force a new fighter. You're more likely to be competing to paint hangars at the local Air Force base, or supply envelopes to your neighborhood Social Security office. On contracts like these, which make up the overwhelming majority of government procurements, design is of less concern. You will receive detailed specifications and the qualified bidder who offers to meet those specifications for the lowest price will, as a general rule, be awarded the contract.

It's also worth noting that bidding will, in all probability, be very competitive. That's because government contracts attract far more competition than most contracts in the private sector. Bidding for a private-sector job, you may be up against only a few other rivals.

In government contracting, depending on what you are bidding on, your competitors may number in the hundreds. They may range from giant corporations to small shops like yours. If you're going to be low bidder in that kind of crowd, you have to play the numbers very carefully indeed.

## Profit

You may be expecting to be able to pad your contract with all kinds of outrageous expenses, come up with arbitrary prices for the final product or service, perhaps even negotiate a deal with a built-in profit margin.

Forget that. Nothing could be further from the truth. Cost-plus-a-percentage contracts, which guarantee a certain profit margin to the contractor regardless of costs, are outlawed by Congress. You may be able to win a bid that includes a certain amount of profit over and above your costs. But you aren't rewarded with extra profit for generating bloated costs.

Judith McDowall, for instance, had to do far more than just tell the government what she would be willing to work for. It took considerable research, including digging up the prices of past winners of toxicological research contracts, before she was able to come up with a bid that would give her both a fair profit and a fair chance for Biotechnical Services to win the award.

That's not to say that adequate profits cannot be made in government contracting. The number of firms that regularly compete for these contracts testifies to the profit potential of government contracting. The point is, the government isn't going to guarantee you a percentage profit. That's up to you, through careful bidding, scrupulous cost cutting, and constant attention to the bottom line.

"More and more, we're stressing quality as distinguished from the use of the sealed bid with low bidder getting the award," adds VanArsdale. "There is enhanced opportunity for a small business with a can-do spirit and a commitment to high quality. But this has never been a good environment for businesses who want to just get by, and it's probably getting worse for them."

## Costs

Don't expect to be able to include a country club membership for yourself along with the billing for any government contract. Government auditors are rigorous and, just as your profit is your concern, so are your perks.

True enough, sometimes questionable items do slip through. You have only to read the business press for a few weeks or months to see word of another scandal large or small concerning questionable billing practices by government contractors. But these cases are usually very large contracts with hard-to-define perimeters of what's allowed and what isn't.

A multiyear, multibillion-dollar contract to design and produce a new guided-missile cruiser, for example, might have room to hold vast chunks of the business overhead generated by a major defense contractor. If you're contracting to repave the driveway at your local VA Hospital, you're going to have to pay your own green fees and play by the rules.

And in government contracting, there are rules in plenty.

## Reasons for Rules

The main source of rules in the government marketing world is something called the Federal Acquisition Regulations (FARs), part of the Code of Federal Regulations. You will become familiar with many of these regulations in the course of reading this book and making your own bids. There are seemingly endless numbers of FARs, covering every aspect of government acquisition. Where they leave off, there is usually another set of government regulations to take up the slack.

Coping with all these rules may sometimes seem like a pointless headache. You may get a little steamed the first time your bid is declared "nonresponsive," or unacceptable, by a contracting officer because of some seemingly minor error such as you submitted it a day, an hour or a minute late, or you sent only three copies instead of four, or you neglected to fill out Block 27 of the umpteenth form included in your bid.

After all, how much difference can it make whether your bid arrives at the contracting office at 12 noon on the day it's due, or at a quarter after? Why is it important not only that you provide the government with the goods or services, but that you provide documents documenting that you documented the delivery?

Be forewarned now, questions like these are likely to occur to you. Seemingly endless requirements for documents and forms are a part of government contracting. When Biotechnical Services sent out its first winning proposal, McDowall remembers being impressed by its size as much as anything.

"There were two volumes," says McDowall. "The technical proposal was one volume and the business proposal was one volume and we have multiple copies of each. Sixteen of the technical, in fact."

Why should you have to follow such rules? The first answer is, it's important to follow the rules because you simply have to. The FARs and other government acquisition rules have the force of law. Violating the most serious in some cases may be a criminal act. In others, it will simply cause you to be declared nonresponsive to the government's solicitation. In other words, you lose out on the chance to even have your bid considered.

If you're going to sell to the government, you're going to have to learn to cross all your *t*'s and dot all your *i*'s—and then go back and check to make sure you didn't miss any.

The overriding reason for the existence of these rules in the first place is simple: fairness. There are two main objectives of all government rules and both relate directly to fairness.

**A Good Deal for Government.** The rules are there, first of all, to make sure the government gets the best deal it can. That's only fair, since it's public money we're spending here, including a portion of the taxes you and your company pay. But the government is a real stickler for getting a good deal in all the details.

When you open the bid documents for an opportunity to sell paint to the government, you'll almost certainly find a reference to a detailed and lengthy list of requirements for the chemical composition of that paint.

If you're selling a painting service, the government will doubtless tell you exactly in what sequence and with what result you'll have to prep and prime the surface, apply the paint and clean it all up afterwards, along with any other services that make up the deal.

The purpose of this is not to drive you crazy, or to give contracting officers a reason to reject your bid. It's to make sure that the government's paint stays stuck on whatever it's meant to cover, for as long as it's supposed to.

In other words, the government wants its money's worth. And in the long run, that's in everybody's best interest.

**Fair Treatment for Bidders.** A second, by no means unimportant, objective of all these rules is to see that all bidders are treated fairly.

In a perfect world, it shouldn't matter that one bidder has an uncle in the Senate, or that another is a lifelong Republican, or that a third plays golf with the contracting officer. In the world we live in, these unfair advantages do sometimes come into play. But it's much less common for a government contract to be awarded on the basis of favoritism or inside information than in other business fields.

Uncertainty can be a problem. Judith McDowall is often happier spending the time and effort to assemble a bid on a private-sector opportunity than she might be on a similar government project. The reason is, she frequently already knows that she's going to win the commercial deal. "Many times we're putting together a proposal and we know basically it's a go," she says. "It's just a matter of negotiating the specifics."

In government contracting, situations in which the sale is a sure thing are the exceptions to the rule. VanArsdale stresses that obtaining inside, nonpublic information about a government contract is a crime. After all, this wouldn't be fair to other bidders who think they have just as good a chance as anybody else. One of the big reasons government contracting is fair is that most decisions are open for all to see.

## An Open World

With its size, variety, and forbidding rules, the government marketplace seems as intimidating to many small firms as, say, selling to the Japanese. But there is yet another big advantage to selling to the government. And it's another plus that all those rules are there to ensure.

That is, openness. Government contracting is one of the few markets where you can find out what your customer wants, in detail, at any time. You can do this by referring to the aforementioned bid documents, studying the government standards and specifications, checking out the applicable FARs, and even by looking at past successful bids for the same product or service.

Documents specifying what the government wants are, generally, available for the asking. Compare that to the cost and delay—not to mention the uncertain value—of customer surveys that purport to tell businesses what private-market buyers want.

The same thing holds when you want to find out how your customer wants to do business. In selling to private buyers, especially large Fortune 500 companies, the hardest parts are figuring out who the decision maker is, guessing who will influence that decision maker, and, finally, what it will take to get the decision you want.

You rarely have these problems in government contracting. Here, the rules of the game are clearly laid out. You can refer to the FARs to learn exactly how the government expects this procurement to take place. The bid documents will generally let you know how the final decision will be made, and what it will take to win the bid.

For example, Judith McDowall knew pretty well what she had to do in order to fulfill the contract for toxicology research, just from having read the solicitation documents. But, having never bid on a government contract before, she wasn't sure exactly what it would take from a financial standpoint.

The government's records of past awards, which she was able to get the government to release, made the situation much clearer. She found data regarding the price named by past winning bidders. "The price information helped a lot," she says, of her efforts to extract data on past contracts. "On price, there wasn't much information that was usable otherwise."

Of course, openness, too, has its limitations. Certain bid advertisements will carry a notation stating that the project is a military or space program with sensitive aspects. In other words, it's secret.

You can't get a look at the bid documents for one of these classified projects without clearance from the Department of Defense. Even with that, you must have a need to know. Usually, these contracts are for things which are obviously secret, such as designing wargames to test the Army's tactical readiness. But they may also cover things such as security guards and even housekeeping services.

## Needs You Can See

One of the wonderful and troublesome things about government contracting is the near-universal existence of standards, specifications, official requirements, and so forth. If you don't meet the specs, you're in trouble. But they are there for anyone to see. And, if you are willing to adjust to meet them—your market just opened wide.

Reference Software found that government standardization was a terrific benefit in marketing its computerized grammar-checkers. In the retail market, a grammar-checking software vendor has to be able to work with dozens of incompatible word processing packages. The government, on the other hand, was largely standardized on a handful of word processing packages, all of which Reference's product, Grammatik, already worked on.

Furthermore, the government had a ready-made, standard set of grammar-checking and other rules which nearly all government writing was supposed to follow. It was no problem to obtain copies of the Government Printing Office Style Manual, the most widely used manual, as well as less widely used writing manuals such as the Army's.

Then says, Reference's Mallett, "We were able to create a government-specific edition of Grammatik. And this is where we really started to see results."

If you don't mind working in the open, you think government deserves a fair shake, and you think you deserve the same chance as anybody else, selling to Uncle Sam is one of the few places you can find exactly that.

## Sweetest Payoff

Some of the biggest companies in the United States were founded or gained a major portion of their growth thanks to government contracts. You don't have to be a military contractor to be a member of that group. Aside from obvious ones like General Dynamics and McDonnell Douglas, that list includes computer companies such as IBM, clothing companies like Haggar, and even Exxon, which lists the U.S. Government as one of its largest customers.

But if government contracting is highly competitive, laden with rules and bureaucracy, open for all to see whatever secrets you may have, and doesn't even guarantee a profit—why does anybody do it? There are several answers to that question.

### Stability

Federal government procurements tend to be insulated from the economic rollercoaster that affects other customers. A big, long-term government contract can provide you with a solid revenue stream upon which to grow through good times and bad.

"It helps to normalize the feast and famine situation that contract organizations face," explains Judith McDowall. "So one of the objectives was to stabilize things and provide a mix of long-term versus short-term projects."

Some types of federal expenditures are actually countercyclical. That is, when economic times are bad and private sector buyers are cutting back, government buyers are likely to be spending more. Sometimes the government does this as a matter of fiscal policy, injecting money into the economy through purchases of goods or services. Other times, federal expenditures rise during bad times because they have to.

A couple of examples of countercyclical opportunities include servicing repossessed property that was purchased with guaranteed government loans, building public housing, and so forth. A careful mix of government business can help you grow while other companies are floundering.

## Security

When you are selling to the U.S. government, your customer has the best credit in the world. If you have a contract from Uncle Sam, you don't need to ask for references or run it by your credit department.

That's not to say that a government contract is as good as money in the bank. You still have to deliver in order to claim your check. And it's not unheard-of for people to have trouble doing that, or even for small subcontractors to run afoul of disputes between the government and prime contractors that have little to do with them.

George Bennett, Jr., built Glacier Partitions & Ceilings Inc., into a going Baltimore-area concern before running afoul of just such a problem. What seemed like a routine subcontracting job painting buildings at a government installation went sour when his payment was hung up, in part, because of a tussle between the prime contractor and the government agency.

The prime, an established company that did hundreds of millions of dollars worth of government business a year, could afford to wait out the dispute. Bennett, out hundreds of thousands of dollars, couldn't. By the time the dispute was settled, it was too late for Glacier.

"Now, basically, I'm out of business," says Bennett.

Things can go wrong in any business, especially one which relies overmuch on one or a few customers. But, suffice it to say, you'll have ample opportunity to dispute any problems you have getting paid. While the government is a demanding customer, you can expect to be treated fairly.

And there are things you can do to make it less likely you will have any problems. If you are subcontracting, check into the history of relations between the government and the prime contractor. If they've been stormy, be sure you have the capitalization to ride out a storm if one blows up.

You also have to make sure that the money has been or is certain to be allocated before actively pursuing any contract. It's not uncommon for bids to be advertised with a telling line to the effect that the project is contingent on funds being allocated for it. Sometimes you may begin researching a possible bid opportunity, only to find out during the process that its prospects of being funded are more speculative than you thought.

That doesn't mean you should forget about the bid. It does mean you need to keep from expending too many resources until Congress or the agency involved has actually set aside the money for this particular program.

And, in the final analysis, checks from Washington rarely fail to clear the bank.

## Size

It's already been noted that Uncle Sam is the world's biggest consumer. What this means to you is that you'll have the opportunity to sell bigger deals to Washington than you might ever sell in the private sector.

It can be a struggle meeting the requirements and winning the bid, true. But because the government buys so much and its needs are so vast, a single contract may dwarf all your other business.

A deal like that can give you the base to grow your business much faster and more securely than you could by depending on commercial contracts.

After landing her first big contract, Judith McDowall had to sit back and decide what kind of company she wanted to be. Did she want to be dominated by government contracts? Or did she want to grow into more commercial work, using the government business as a base?

"From a profit point of view that's something we're discussing more and more, what is the appropriate mix," says McDowall. While she recognizes the stability and other values of a government contract, she also recognizes that bidding is a strenuous and uncertain process that generates lots of costs on its own. Profit margins in government work also tend to be lower than on commercial jobs.

"Writing services are not perceived as a particularly high value-added service," McDowall comments wryly, "at least in the government."

So, she's trying to win more commercial work to balance out the federal jobs. But, she admits, trying not to give too much of your business to a single customer is a nice problem to have.

## Sophistication

During the course of fulfilling a government contract, you may be able to develop technology, skills, or processes that you can turn into highly marketable items in the commercial arena.

The classic cases of this are well-known consumer products like Teflon nonstick cooking surfaces and Tang instant breakfast drink. Both of them had their start as part of government-funded projects in the space program. Later, they went on to considerable commercial success.

When it comes to many types of basic research, the government or government-funded organizations are the only possible customers. In fact, the Department of Defense is required by law to stimulate technological innovation among small high-technology firms under the Small Business Innovation Research program. Who else is likely to pay for a study evaluating the carcinogenic effect of sodium fluoride on laboratory animals? Yet contracts just that esoteric, and more, are let all the time by government buyers.

Many government contracts pay you while you develop or perfect skills that are much closer to being marketable than the far-out talents listed above. That's not to say you can bid on a government contract on a subject about which you know nothing, then learn it from the ground up while the government foots the bill. But if you have most of the skills needed, have prepared an attractive proposal compared to your rivals, and show an ability to learn what you need, you may be able to substantially improve your mastery of those skills on the job.

Often, government contracts become much more complex during the course of their performance than anybody expected at the outset. Over the life of a contract, you may be led into some areas you never expected to visit, and leave better off than you came.

## Status

As a stable company with good long-term prospects based on revenues from government business, you become a much more attractive employer. You'll be able to offer prospective employees the opportunity to work in a demanding, up-to-the-minute environment, with the added bonus of financial security.

In addition to attracting the best employees, you will find your financial appeal greatly enhanced when you sign your first government contract. Understandably, bank officials and other lenders are much more receptive to a company whose sales are backed by Uncle Sam.

Finally, there is a good deal of prestige associated with being good enough for government work. The government is often more stringent in their requirements than the commercial market. Government products may be required to operate under wartime mission scenarios in a variety of different environmental conditions. Uncle Sam is big and hungry and at times may seem indiscriminate in what he buys. But much of that image is a reflection of the admittedly stodgy and inefficient government bureaucracy.

And a lot of that image is out of date. "It's different," says SBA's VanArsdale. "It's changing along with the general shift in the business environment."

What that means is, increasingly, you need the same advanced skills to compete, whether you're in private business or government contracting.

"The things I hear corporate people talking about are total quality management, high-quality, long-term relationships, and vendors who have a high-technology capability in terms of management," says VanArsdale. "I think government is shifting that way too."

## Sanity

In a world where things are moving so fast and in so many directions that it sometimes seems impossible to even track them all, much less respond, government contracting provides something of an oasis.

That's not to say you can take a leisurely approach to selling to Uncle Sam. Often, you will learn of a bid opportunity with barely enough time remaining before the bid deadline for you to assemble your proposal and get it in. Late nights and early mornings are likely to be the rule in government contracting.

But government contracting has a steady rhythm to it that many businesses don't. And, despite the plethora of regulations and forms, there is room for the human side of business here. In fact, says, Daniel J. O'Brien, national director of emerging business services for Coopers & Lybrand, getting to know the humans who will actually use your product or service is one of the best ways to sell to the government.

"If you want to succeed in this area, ask questions," O'Brien advises. "The people who seem not to do well are the people who get the solicitation, answer in a mechanical way, and make stupid mistakes like not following the bureaucratic guidelines. They never pick up the phone and ask questions of the contracting officer."

The SBA's VanArsdale cautions that personal contact in government dealings does not play the same role it does in the private sector.

"Networking is important here not because you're going to get any kind of edge or advance information," he says. "That's unusual and a criminal act when it occurs. But it is important, because you get a feel for the agency and an appreciation for how they're going to think when they're making decisions."

Those who win in government contracting manage to walk both sides of that equation, fulfilling all the arcane requirements, while still remembering that their goods and services are going to be used by people, and it is people who will approve the purchase.

And that is government contracting. It's a vast, intricate, often perplexing opportunity that requires dedication and skill to exploit.

Government contracting is no place for the weak, the careless, or the faint of heart. It requires a mastery of detail and an ability to plan long term and analyze business propositions that is nearly unique. But if you can succeed and survive here, rest assured that you can compete anywhere else.

# 2 Starting the Sale

## Potential Government Markets

Besides being the globe's biggest and hungriest consumer, Uncle Sam is also the most complex. The number of government buyers is almost as varied as the number of things the government buys.

In addition to the huge buyers like the Department of Defense and General Services Administration in Washington, D.C., there are hundreds of lesser-known government departments and agencies that buy from businesses small and large. These range from the Soil Conservation Service to the U.S. Nuclear Regulatory Commission.

Not all government contracts are awarded by someone in Washington, either. Many of the thousands of government installations scattered over the country and, indeed, the world buy products and services directly from local suppliers. Often these potential buyers are obscure. The Rolla Research Center of the Bureau of Mines, in Rolla, Mo., the procurement office of the nearest Army, Air Force, or Navy base, or any of thousands of other government offices all have needs and money to spend.

Your chance to win these contracts is, much of the time, every bit as good as a bigger firm's. In some cases, thanks to laws mandating built-in bias for small firms, it's better. But whether small or large, successful government contractors must know and follow the unique rules of selling to the government. In this chapter we will examine the types of government contracts, how to become a bidder, and the role of small business in government contracting.

## ...racts

...st and sometimes bewildering array of government ...t two basic methods of government purchasing— ... competitive procurement. The direct purchase ... is frequently used for procurements valued at $25,000 or less. In this case the government buyer may call you on the phone or issue a simple written Request for Quotation (RFQ). The government agency then issues a purchase order to the successful quoter for specified goods and services at a specified price, deliverable at a specified time. We're not going to concern ourselves with the direct purchase method in this book, as it operates very much like commercial purchasing.

The second type of purchasing is the competitive procurement process. We're devoting our attention to this manner of procurement because of its intricacies and its vast difference from private industry bidding practices. Competitive procurement is done through either invitations for bid or requests for proposal.

### Invitation for Bid

An Invitation for Bid (IFB) uses the sealed bid process for procuring goods and services. In an IFB the government must state exactly what it intends to procure so that all bidders—or offerors as they're known in contracting parlance—are bidding on the same requirements and competing at the same level. Because of the requirement for a precise description of what the government wants to buy, the IFB process is most commonly used for straightforward items like stationery, commodities, simple services, and construction.

Though relatively simple, IFBs have their own rigorous protocol. Each invitation for bid contains a submission deadline and your offer must be received before the date and time specified in the IFB for it to be considered. Your offer must also be for the exact goods and services specified in the IFB. Any deviations will be cause for rejection of the offer.

The actual award is simple. The government opens the IFB at the time and place specified and reads each offer aloud. Award is then made to the bid with the lowest price that meets the requirements. Again the key phrase is "meets the requirements of the IFB" because once the bid is opened modifications are generally not allowed.

### Request for Proposal

A Request for Proposal (RFP) is usually issued by the government when the goods or services being procured cannot be defined in enough detail to issue an IFB. Also an RFP may be issued when the buying agency feels that negotiation may be necessary. The key distinction is that the government doesn't know exactly what it wants, or how you can fulfill its need.

From your perspective, the big difference is that you have an opportunity to expound on your capabilities in a give-and-take process with the government when responding to an RFP. You may have more than one chance to submit your offer to the government—in essence, an opportunity to negotiate instead of making a flat offer, as with an IFB. Large, complex contracts for both military weapons systems and civilian goods and services are almost always done through RFPs.

An RFP usually requires more effort on your part than an IFB. You'll probably have to describe in writing—and at some length—your approach and methodology for accomplishing the tasks defined in the RFP. That's not all bad. It leaves room for you to emphasize to some degree your unique resources and methods, which may give you a competitive edge.

RFPs are not opened in public. These proposals usually go through a rigorous review process by the buying agency behind closed doors. This review is often performed by a team of experts in the fields related to the goods or services being solicited in the RFP. You can attend a bid opening for an IFB and find out immediately how you fared. But if you offer on an RFP, you'll be notified through mail, phone call, or fax whether you won or lost.

## How to Become a Bidder

Becoming a bidder for government procurements is a simple although somewhat time-consuming process because of the paperwork that has to be shuffled back and forth. An understanding of government paperwork and how it is processed is essential to marketing your product. Doing business with the government requires not only that you market your product but that you actively seek out the market for your product.

Marketing for government business is quite different from marketing to regular consumers. You won't do any media advertising or large scale campaigns. Instead, you'll work by contacting government buying agencies, networking with other government contractors, and reviewing certain publications and periodicals for upcoming opportunities. These three legs are the tripod upon which your government marketing program will stand.

## Contacting Buyers

In order to make a bid on any contract, sooner or later you'll have to get a copy of the solicitation notice, which is nothing more than a document stating what the government wants and when it wants it. To receive solicitations for goods and services from a government buying agency, you must either be on that particular agency's mailing list or find out about the solicitation and ask for a copy. In this section we will deal with getting your firm on a mailing list, which will ensure that you automatically learn about some—though not all—chances to make a sale.

To get on a specific government agency's mailing list you must complete the necessary application forms used by that agency. Now is as good a time as any to state that the ability to accurately fill out numerous and detailed forms is an essential and significant part of doing business with the government. If you don't have that ability, you need to gain it or find somebody in your company who already has it.

"You have to follow all the instructions—all the instructions," emphasizes one small business expert at a Big Six accounting firm. "If you do not, you can lose the job."

Mailing list application forms are generally easy to fill out and fairly standardized. However, as each agency may have its own methods and forms or at least a modification of the standard methods, it is best to write the agency you've targeted and ask for its forms. Figure 2-1 illustrates a form letter that may be used to contact government agencies.

Of course, you have to know who to write to first. An excellent source of names and addresses for government agencies is the *U.S. Government Purchasing and Sales Directory* published by the U.S. Government Printing Office. (See Sources for Additional Information at the end of the book.) This directory is often available through your local Small Business Administration office, sometimes at no charge, or at your local Government Book Store. Either of these offices can be located by consulting your telephone book blue pages or calling directory information.

In the purchasing and sales directory you will find a listing of products and services bought by major military and civilian federal agencies along with a listing of the names and addresses of those agencies. You simply look up the listing for whatever it is you have to sell, cross-index to find which government agencies bought it in the past, and write to that agency. State and local agencies can usually be contacted by writing to your state, city, or county office of procurement.

WE Manufacture
Crown Plaza
Somewhere, US 10020

August 8, 1993

Office of Procurement
Government Buying Agency
124 Main Street
Anywhere, US 10131

Dear Procurement Officer:

Please allow me to introduce our company. WE Manufacture is a small business that produces fabricated sheetmetal parts. We would like to bid on government procurements that require such items.

Please send me the necessary forms to be included on your bidders list. If you have any questions concerning our company, feel free to contact me.

Sincerely,

John Doe
Government Marketing Representative

**Figure 2-1.** Sample letter for making initial government contact.

**The Solicitation Mailing List Application.** The basic form used by federal government agencies is Standard Form (SF) 129, *Solicitation Mailing List Application*. You'll almost certainly receive it or a variant in the return mail after writing to a buying agency. This form, illustrated in Figure 2-2, is self-explanatory and has instructions printed on the back. It should take just a few minutes to fill out.

**SOLICITATION MAILING LIST APPLICATION**

1. TYPE OF APPLICATION ☐ INITIAL ☐ REVISION | 2. DATE | FORM APPROVED OMB NO. 3090-0009

NOTE—Please complete all items on this form. Insert N/A in items not applicable. See reverse for Instructions.

3. NAME AND ADDRESS OF FEDERAL AGENCY TO WHICH FORM IS SUBMITTED *(Include ZIP code)*

4. NAME AND ADDRESS OF APPLICANT *(Include county and ZIP code)*

5. TYPE OF ORGANIZATION *(Check one)*

☐ INDIVIDUAL ☐ NON-PROFIT ORGANIZATION

☐ PARTNERSHIP ☐ CORPORATION, INCORPORATED UNDER THE LAWS OF THE STATE OF:

6. ADDRESS TO WHICH SOLICITATIONS ARE TO BE MAILED *(If different than Item 4)*

7. NAMES OF OFFICERS, OWNERS, OR PARTNERS

| A. PRESIDENT | B. VICE PRESIDENT | C. SECRETARY |
|---|---|---|
| D. TREASURER | E. OWNERS OR PARTNERS | |

8. AFFILIATES OF APPLICANT *(Names, locations and nature of affiliation. See definition on reverse.)*

9. PERSONS AUTHORIZED TO SIGN OFFERS AND CONTRACTS IN YOUR NAME *(Indicate if agent)*

| NAME | OFFICIAL CAPACITY | TELE. NO. *(Include area code)* |
|---|---|---|
| | | |
| | | |
| | | |

10. IDENTIFY EQUIPMENT, SUPPLIES, AND/OR SERVICES ON WHICH YOU DESIRE TO MAKE AN OFFER *(See attached Federal agency's supplemental listing and instructions, if any)*

11A. SIZE OF BUSINESS *(See definitions on reverse)*

☐ SMALL BUSINESS *(If checked, complete items 11B and 11C)* ☐ OTHER THAN SMALL BUSINESS

11B. AVERAGE NUMBER OF EMPLOYEES *(Including affiliates)* FOR FOUR PRECEDING CALENDAR QUARTERS

11C. AVERAGE ANNUAL SALES OR RECEIPTS FOR PRECEDING THREE FISCAL YEARS

$

12. TYPE OF OWNERSHIP *(See definitions on reverse) (Not applicable for other than small businesses)*

☐ DISADVANTAGED BUSINESS ☐ WOMAN-OWNED BUSINESS

13. TYPE OF BUSINESS *(See definitions on reverse)*

☐ MANUFACTURER OR PRODUCER ☐ REGULAR DEALER *(Type 1)* ☐ CONSTRUCTION CONCERN ☐ SURPLUS DEALER

☐ SERVICE ESTABLISHMENT ☐ REGULAR DEALER *(Type 2)* ☐ RESEARCH AND DEVELOPMENT

14. DUNS NO. *(If available)*

15. HOW LONG IN PRESENT BUSINESS?

| 16. FLOOR SPACE *(Square feet)* | | 17. NET WORTH | |
|---|---|---|---|
| A. MANUFACTURING | B. WAREHOUSE | A. DATE | B. AMOUNT $ |

18. SECURITY CLEARANCE *(If applicable, check highest clearance authorized)*

| FOR | TOP SECRET | SECRET | CONFIDENTIAL | C. NAMES OF AGENCIES WHICH GRANTED SECURITY CLEARANCES *(Include dates)* |
|---|---|---|---|---|
| A. KEY PERSONNEL | | | | |
| B. PLANT ONLY | | | | |

CERTIFICATION — I certify that information supplied herein *(Including all pages attached)* is correct and that neither the applicant nor any person *(Or concern)* in any connection with the applicant as a principal or officer, so far as is known, is now debarred or otherwise declared ineligible by any agency of the Federal Government from making offers for furnishing materials, supplies, or services to the Government or any agency thereof.

| 19. NAME AND TITLE OF PERSON AUTHORIZED TO SIGN *(Type or print)* | 20. SIGNATURE | 21. DATE SIGNED |
|---|---|---|
| | | |

NSN 7540-01-152-8086
PREVIOUS EDITIONS UNUSABLE

129-106

STANDARD FORM 129 (REV. 10-83)
Prescribed by GSA
FAR (48 CFR) 53.214(c)

**Figure 2-2.** Solicitation Mailing List Application (Standard Form 129).

It should be noted that the various agencies use different coding methods for identifying the goods and services being provided. Therefore, the standard mailing list application form is sometimes modified by the government agency, usually in Block 10 where you identify the products and services you wish to offer. Some agencies have supplemental forms you have to fill out in addition to an SF 129. For instance, the U.S. Postal Service has its supplemental Form 7429, while the Department of Defense uses its own Form 558-1 supplement. These additional forms are also simple and easy to complete.

Send the completed forms to the address given in the instructions along with a cover letter. Your cover letter should request that the agency acknowledge receiving your application and tell you what product mailing lists your firm has been entered on. In all phases of government contracting, it's important to remember that you aren't the only one who can make mistakes. Continually monitor the government buyers you are dealing with to make sure that their mistakes, or the mistakes of others, don't wind up hurting you. Start now by making sure you're on the right mailing lists.

This is also an opportune time to forward any company literature on your products and services. One copy is sufficient as the literature can be used only for information purposes.

Note that getting your firm on the solicitation mailing list is just part of your marketing triad. It does not even mean you will be contacted every time there is a need for your product. The government method for use of the mailing list is to randomly select a number of firms and mail the solicitation to them. This is why it is important to actively pursue other marketing methods.

**The SBA Rep.** In addition to contacting specific government agencies, you should also get in touch with your local Small Business Administration Commercial Market Representative. This person has a wealth of knowledge that can help your general business affairs. The SBA is also where you go to learn about government-sponsored seminars and procurement conferences, where you can learn even more about marketing to the government.

Your SBA representative can also arrange for you to be listed on the Procurement Automated Source System (PASS), which is a computer database that serves as a referral center and inventory of small businesses seeking government work. Government buyers and prime contractors can use PASS to locate potential small business suppliers. You'll be indexed by the following:

Descriptive keywords that identify a product or service, such as *software, delivery,* or *training.*

Federal Supply Codes (FSC), which are used to categorize federal suppliers by their specific product. If your FSC is 1620, for example, you are a supplier of aircraft landing gear components.

Standard Industrial Classification (SIC) codes, which are used to categorize manufacturers by their specialty. For instance, SIC code 352 identifies manufacturers of farm and garden machinery and equipment.

DUNS number. DUNS stands for Data Universal Numbering System. The FAR requires that each government contractor be assigned a number to identify each plant or location.

Geographic region, such as East, West, Southwest, etc.

Getting listed on PASS requires you to fill out a brief form that takes just a few minutes. Once you're listed, it will be much easier for potential customers to find you. Again, it's just part of the comprehensive government marketing campaign you'll need to succeed, but it's an important one.

## Networking with Other Government Contractors

Marketing to the government isn't all done through letters and computer terminals. Person-to-person networking is another vital part of your marketing program. You can meet other contractors at sealed-bid openings, contracting seminars, and trade shows for your industry or for government marketing in general. Get to know as many contractors as possible.

Successful contractors often have work to farm out—possibly to you. Even if you're direct competitors, you may be able to team up on contracts too large for either of you to handle on your own. Subcontract and joint-venture opportunities may relieve you of the cumbersome paperwork involved with government contracting and allow you to concentrate on the activities you profit from the most.

Making contacts isn't all that difficult. Even the biggest prime contractors have good reasons for wanting to get to know you. The Department of Defense has a requirement that prime contractors and subcontractors who receive contracts valued over $500,000 ($1,000,000 for construction) establish plans and goals for subcontracting with small and small disadvantaged businesses. An excellent source for identifying these major prime contractors is the *Small Business Subcontracting*

*Directory* published by the U.S. Government Printing Office. This directory is available at your local Government Book Store.

Each Small Business Administration office also keeps a directory of major prime contractors for their region. In it you will find listed alphabetically by state the name and telephone number of the prime's small business liaison officer (SBLO), whom you should contact. Figure 2-3 illustrates a form letter that may be used to contact a SBLO. Your local library also has reference books that identify manufacturers and suppliers by their products to help you pick companies to contact.

Just because you're a subcontractor doesn't mean you get a subpar share of the rewards.

"The subcontracting opportunities are where the small business can really make a killing," says one government business consultant. "Most of the bid preparation costs are borne by the prime contractor. The subs just sort of sit back and supply information and support the prime and don't take on a lot of the risk."

## Reviewing Publications and Periodicals

Government contracts are let every business day of the year, so you need regular and, in some cases, frequent updates to keep track of openings. That's why publications and periodicals are another rich source of government business opportunities.

**Newspapers and Journals.** Invitations for bid on local projects can often be found in the classified advertising section of the daily newspaper. Your metropolitan area may also have a weekly business newspaper or journal that lists IFBs. You can find out about such publications by contacting your local chamber of commerce. Nationally, financial newspapers such as *The Wall Street Journal* publish contract awards of significant size.

While you may learn about an award after the fact, this does not mean that all the pieces of the puzzle have been put together. Your contribution may, in fact, be the missing piece the award winner is looking for. Opportunities may still exist for your products and services to win you a place as a subcontractor.

***The Commerce Business Daily.*** Probably the most complete source for finding out about federal government procurements is the *Commerce Business Daily*. The CBD, as it is known, is available from the Superintendent of Documents, Government Printing Office,

WE Manufacture
Crown Plaza
Somewhere, US 10020

August 8, 1993

Small Business Liaison Officer
Prime Contractor
124 Main Street
Anywhere, US 10131

Dear Small Business Liaison Officer:

I am writing to you to introduce our company and request information on participation in your small business program. WE Manufacture is a small firm that produces fabricated sheetmetal parts. Our experience includes fabrication of a variety of parts for the transportation and manufacturing industries. I have enclosed a brochure for your review.

We are interested in participating in government projects with prime contractors such as you. If you desire further information on our company, feel free to contact me.

Sincerely,

John Doe
Government Marketing Representative

Enclosure

**Figure 2-3.** Sample letter for contacting the prime contractor.

Washington, DC 20402-9317. All federal government buying agencies are required by Federal Acquisition Regulation to synopsize in the CBD any proposed competitive contracts expected to exceed $25,000, any proposed noncompetitive contracts expected to exceed $10,000, and any contract awards in excess of $25,000.

The CBD's publisher, the Department of Commerce, has subtitled this publication as "a daily list of U.S. Government procurement invitations, contract awards, subcontracting leads, sales of surplus property and foreign business opportunities." And the CBD certainly can fulfill even that hefty promise—if you use it to its full potential.

**Prospecting with the CBD.** Fortunately, the CBD is relatively easy to follow. It is structured in five different sections: U.S. Government Procurements, Contract Awards, Special Notices, Foreign Government Standards, and Surplus Property Sales. The first two sections contain subsections for Services, Supplies, Equipment, and Material. The subsections are further divided by specialty codes such as Architect-Engineer Services, Aircraft Components and Accessories, etc. Here is a brief explanation of each of the five major sections in the CBD:

1. *U.S. Government Procurements.* This section, which takes up most of the CBD, is where you will find a brief synopsis of products or services that are being sought for purchase, along with the name, address, and point of contact at the buying agency. You can write to this agency for the solicitation document which will provide a detailed description of the product or service. If a synopsis catches your eye, read it carefully to see whether you have any problems with the stated requirements. If you have any questions, call the point of contact listed in the synopsis.

2. *Contract Awards.* This section of the CBD provides a listing by product or service of contract awards. The list includes the dollar amount of the contract and the names and addresses of the recipients. It's fertile ground for subcontracting prospects. You can farm it by writing to the contacts shown and requesting information.

It is not uncommon for a prime contractor to bid a job not knowing for sure who it will subcontract work to. Perhaps this contractor is in a town just a few miles down the road from you but is not aware that you can provide a product it needs. It could be that the contractor was contemplating using a source in another part of the country. Imagine the prime contractor's interest in you—and in supporting the local community, reducing transportation costs, and being able to monitor subcontractor activities in person rather than from afar!

3. *Special Notices.* This section provides information on upcoming conferences where businesses can meet with the government to discuss what they have to offer and what the government needs. These conferences provide excellent chances to meet government buyers and network with other contractors. They often feature seminars or workshops that can help you understand the finer aspects of government business.

4. *Foreign Government Standards.* This section lists notices of proposed changes in foreign standards and certification systems which may effect U.S. exports. This isn't likely to affect you unless you are planning to pursue business with foreign governments.

5. *Surplus Property Sales.* This section lists all public sales of surplus property. This is the flip side of the government business coin, one that probably won't concern you as someone who wants to sell to the government. But if you have a used car business on the side, this is where you will find notices regarding the sale of surplus vehicles.

One thing that cannot be overemphasized is that you will have to go out and find a market for your goods or services, it will not come to you. While we have listed three effective methods for accomplishing this task—bidding lists, networking, and publications—it always helps to continuously look for other ways. If you know you will be in the area of a government buying agency, contact the small business representative prior to your trip and arrange to meet with this individual. While the representative cannot actively market your product or service for you, if the reps know you exist they can provide a referral when asked.

## Role of Small Business in Government Contracting

You may think you're at a disadvantage compared to giant companies in contracting with the even more gigantic federal government. But actually the federal government actively encourages its buyers to deal with small businesses. There are regulations that require buying agencies to look at each procurement to see if it should be set aside for small business. As we have discussed, there are also regulations that require big businesses to establish a subcontracting plan and utilize small businesses. The Small Business Administration also actively reviews upcoming procurement to make recommendations for utilizing small businesses.

## Small Business Administration

In 1953, Congress passed the Small Business Act which established the Small Business Administration. The SBA, then and now, is tasked with working with federal buying agencies and prime contractors to encourage them to use small businesses as much as possible. In 1978 Congress passed Public Law 95-507, which revised the Small Business Act of 1953 and provided an even stronger commitment to the use of small business in government procurement.

These two laws, as implemented by government buyers, mean that you have a good shot at your piece of the government contracting pie. For example, the Department of Defense (DoD) is the major buying branch of the federal government. The DoD alone accounted for $149 billion of the $210 billion worth of contract actions in fiscal year 1991. Of that $147 billion nearly $20 billion was awarded to small business concerns as prime contractors. Another $22 billion was awarded to small businesses as subcontractors to prime contractors. That amounts to nearly one-third of the money spent by the DoD—20 percent of the total fiscal expenditures for 1991—rung up in small business receipts.

## Who Qualifies as a Small Business

What is the definition of a small business and who determines if you are one? The most common definition of a small business is the one you will find on the back of the SF129 Solicitation Mailing List Application. It reads:

> A small business concern for the purposes of Government procurement is a concern, including its affiliates, which is independently owned and operated, is not dominant in the field of operation in which it is competing for Government contracts and can further qualify under the criteria concerning number of employees, average annual receipts, or other criteria, as prescribed by the Small Business Administration. (See Code of Federal Regulations, Title 13, Part 121, as amended, which contains detailed industry definitions and related procedures.)

In short, the SBA decides who qualifies as a small business. The precise definition may differ across industries. Hypothetically, a landscaping company with 1000 employees might qualify as big, while a similarly sized shipbuilder would be considered small. You can get the details for your industry by contacting your SBA field office. Also, solicitation documents for a particular contract will often clear up any ambiguities by establishing a specific requirement by size and gross annual receipts.

## Types of Small Business Ownership

Among small businesses there are two types of ownership which merit mentioning. These are disadvantaged businesses and women-owned businesses. Again we take our definitions from the back of the SF129 Solicitation Mailing List Application.

A disadvantaged business is:

> Any business concern (1) which is at least 51 percent owned by one or more socially and economically disadvantaged individuals; or, in the case of any publicly owned business, at least 51 percent of the stock of which is owned by one or more socially and economically disadvantaged individuals, and (2) whose management and daily business operations are controlled by one or more such individuals.

A women-owned business is:

> A business that is at least 51 percent owned by a woman or women who are U.S. citizens and who also control and operate the business.

If you recognize yourself in either of these descriptions, you may be singled out to receive solicitations that have been designated for disadvantaged and women-owned businesses only.

## Small, Disadvantaged Businesses [8(a) Qualifiers]

In 1968 the SBA began a contracting and business development program which derives its authority from Section 8(a) of the Small Business Act of 1953. Under the 8(a) Program the SBA acts as a prime contractor to the federal government and subcontracts the work to small businesses. This program is designed to help socially and economically disadvantaged businesses that are in need of work to make the business survive. Applications for the 8(a) program are reviewed on a per case basis using the following criteria:

1. *Ownership.* The business must be at least 51 percent owned by an individual(s) who is a citizen of the United States and determined to be socially and economically disadvantaged.

2. *Social Disadvantage.* Individuals who have been subjected to racial or ethnic prejudice or cultural bias without regard to individual qualities. This includes several groups of people such as Black Americans, Hispanic Americans, and Native Americans.
3. *Economic Disadvantage.* To be economically disadvantaged you must first be socially disadvantaged. Then your ability to compete in the free-enterprise system, as compared to same or similar businesses in a competitive market who are not socially disadvantaged, must be impaired due to diminished capital and credit opportunities.
4. *Control and Management.* The business must be controlled by socially and economically disadvantaged individuals who participate in the daily management and operation of the company.
5. *Size Standard.* The business must meet the size standard determined by the SBA.
6. *Potential for Success.* The business must be determined to be capable of performing subcontracts with a reasonable potential for success in competition in the private sector.

Your local SBA office can help you with application and qualification if you feel you meet the requirements of this category. It should be noted that qualifying as an 8(a) contractor does not guarantee you work, and you must have been in business for at least two years before you can apply. But if you are a member of the 8(a) group, you could have a strong advantage.

"We see that community growing in market share and doing very, very well," says one Washington, D.C., consultant who specializes in government contracting for small electronics companies. "In fiscal year 1990, the last year we had complete numbers, the 8(a) community took 8 percent of the total market, which is very high in relation to what they represent in the vendor community."

## Small Business Set-Aside

Sometimes a procurement of goods or services is restricted to small businesses. This is referred to as a small business set-aside. If the government can reasonably expect that two or more small businesses can meet the requirements for a good or service, and provide a fair and reasonable price, or in other words that small business competition exists, the contracting officer may determine the procurement to be a set-aside.

There may also be small business set-asides that are restricted to small disadvantaged business firms, or Section 8(a) business firms. If you qualify as one of these firms (using the definition given above), it may well be that boost you need to make your company a success. Public law mandates the Department of Defense to reserve 5 percent of its procurement dollars for small disadvantaged businesses. That figure amounted to 7.5 billion dollars in fiscal year 1991.

# 3
# Inside the Big Brown Envelope

## When to Expect the Bid Envelope

It will not be a surprise to you to learn that, in contracting as elsewhere, the wheels of government grind slowly. Your wheels, on the other hand, are supposed to grind a bit faster.

In most cases, you will learn about a bid opportunity by a notice in the *Commerce Business Daily*. If you're on a mailing list, you may get prior notification or you may get a solicitation in the mail without requesting it. Note that the government mails solicitations for upcoming bid opportunities to a random selection of companies on the mailing list. So you can't expect to receive a bid notification just because of the fact that you're on a mailing list.

When you learn about a bid opportunity through a CBD notice, you may have 30 days or less to obtain the bid documents, prepare your offer, and submit your response. You will have to act quickly.

If you request bid documents and the published due date approaches while your mail box remains empty, don't panic. But don't sit on your hands either. Give the government a reasonable amount of time to mail the documents, then contact the office listed in the CBD announcement and inquire as to its whereabouts.

Solicitations are often postponed for all kinds of reasons. They may even be canceled. The government is supposed to let bidders on the solicitation mailing list know when solicitations are postponed or canceled but they may not do so, especially if the solicitation was canceled before it was issued. The buying agency may just place another ad in the CBD to let bidders know it was canceled.

The point of contact listed in the CBD announcement should be able to tell you whether your solicitation has gotten pushed onto a back burner—or completely off the stove.

## When the Envelope Arrives

Bid documents usually arrive without fanfare in a big brown envelope in the regular mail. Sometimes the government may have a sense of urgency in making this procurement and may send it via some form of express mail or overnight delivery. But most of the time all you need to do by way of exercising suitable vigilance is to keep an eye on your mailbox (and your calendar, to make sure there has not been some slipup).

Once you receive the package, your first step should be to open it and take an inventory of everything that is inside the envelope. That means making a list of the major documents and their various components.

There are a couple of places in the documents where you will find a list of everything that should be in the solicitation. We'll tell you where these lists are and how to read them in the section on Standard Form 33 later in this chapter. For now, you need to know that if you discover anything at all missing, you should immediately contact the person identified in the bid document as the information point of contact and request the missing materials.

If something is supposed to be there, you need it to make an intelligent bid, or to make the intelligent choice not to bid. They could be hard copy blueprints, microfiche blueprints, purchase description, statement of work, contract data requirements list, technical manuals, or any number of other documents.

Once you've made a list of the contents, make a copy of each document. Then file the originals in a safe place away from the copies. There's a reason for this. As the process of bidding progresses you will find that papers get delegated to different individuals or get misplaced, which may require that you obtain another copy. Once the government starts the clock running on a bid they will not delay it to get you a copy of a document you have already received. If you have your own backup copies, you won't need to miss a step if something gets lost.

## The Bid Documents

### The Covering Letter or Form

The bid package may contain a letter from an administrative officer or perhaps a DD Form 1707 (Information to Offerors or Quoters). Read these carefully as they could contain information that is not found in the actual bid document but is of great importance to your firm.

This information may include whether the bid is unrestricted and open to full competition from both large and small businesses alike, or whether and what percentage of the bid is set aside for small businesses or other favored concerns. In other words, this letter or form could tell you whether you have a leg up on the competition for this contract.

The back of DD Form 1707 may be used when a bidder chooses not to respond to a bid. You do not have to fill this out if you don't want to bid, but it is not a bad idea, especially if you decide you want to be maintained on the mailing list for future procurements. Agencies purge their mailing lists from time to time, and if you are an inactive bidder, you could be risking missing out on future opportunities.

### Standard Form 33

The next form you should look for is Standard Form 33 (SF33), Solicitation, Offer and Award, which should be the top page of the bid document. (Like all the myriad government forms you will be using, it is clearly identified on the lower edge.) The government does use other documents such as SF18, Request for Quotations; SF1442, Solicitation, Offer and Award (Construction, Alteration, or Repair); and DD-1155, Order for Supplies or Services/Request for Quotations. Construction companies, for instance, won't see the SF33, but the SF1442 instead. All these forms are somewhat different. However, SF33 is the most common form and the one we will concentrate on for analysis of the bid document.

At first sight SF 33 looks like a cluttered mess, about as appealing as a tax return. (See Figure 3-1.) But there is a lot of information to be recorded here and the form does make sense if you look at each section separately. This particular form is divided into four sections: administration, solicitation, offer, and award. Each square or block where information is to be entered has a number, which we will use to discuss the form and how to fill it out. The blocks also, in most cases, have explana-

**SOLICITATION, OFFER AND AWARD**

1. THIS CONTRACT IS A RATED ORDER UNDER DPAS (15 CFR 350) ▶ RATING | PAGE 1 OF 24 PAGES

2. CONTRACT NO. | 3. SOLICITATION NO. RFP 91-6 | 4. TYPE OF SOLICITATION ☐ SEALED BID (IFB) ☒ NEGOTIATED (RFP) | 5. DATE ISSUED 11/27/91 | 6. REQUISITION/PURCHASE NO.

7. ISSUED BY CODE

Federal Election Commission
999 E Street, N.W.
Washington, D.C. 20463

8. ADDRESS OFFER TO *(If other than Item 7)*

NOTE: In sealed bid solicitations "offer" and "offeror" mean "bid" and "bidder".

**SOLICITATION**

9. Sealed offers in original and 3 copies for furnishing the supplies or services in the Schedule will be received at the place specified in Item 8, or if handcarried, in the depository located in Room 819 until 12:00N *(Hour)* local time 12/27/91 *(Date)*

CAUTION — LATE Submissions, Modifications, and Withdrawals: See Section L, Provision No. 52.214-7 or 52.215-10. All offers are subject to all terms and conditions contained in this solicitation.

10. FOR INFORMATION CALL: ▶ A. NAME | B. TELEPHONE NO. *(Include area code)* *(NO COLLECT CALLS)*

11. TABLE OF CONTENTS

| (√) | SEC. | DESCRIPTION | PAGE(S) | (√) | SEC. | DESCRIPTION | PAGE(S) |
|---|---|---|---|---|---|---|---|
| | | PART I — THE SCHEDULE | | | | PART II — CONTRACT CLAUSES | |
| X | A | SOLICITATION/CONTRACT FORM | 1 | X | I | CONTRACT CLAUSES | 9 |
| X | B | SUPPLIES OR SERVICES AND PRICES/COSTS | 2 | | | PART III — LIST OF DOCUMENTS, EXHIBITS AND OTHER ATTACH. | |
| X | C | DESCRIPTION/SPECS./WORK STATEMENT | 3 | | J | LIST OF ATTACHMENTS | |
| | D | PACKAGING AND MARKING | | | | PART IV — REPRESENTATIONS AND INSTRUCTIONS | |
| | E | INSPECTION AND ACCEPTANCE | | | | | |
| X | F | DELIVERIES OR PERFORMANCE | 6 | X | K | REPRESENTATIONS, CERTIFICATIONS AND OTHER STATEMENTS OF OFFERORS | 11 |
| X | G | CONTRACT ADMINISTRATION DATA | 7 | X | L | INSTRS., CONDS., AND NOTICES TO OFFERORS | 20 |
| | H | SPECIAL CONTRACT REQUIREMENTS | | X | M | EVALUATION FACTORS FOR AWARD | 24 |

**OFFER** *(Must be fully completed by offeror)*

NOTE: Item 12 does not apply if the solicitation includes the provisions at 52.214-16, Minimum Bid Acceptance Period.

12. In compliance with the above, the undersigned agrees, if this offer is accepted within ______ calendar days *(60 calendar days unless a different period is inserted by the offeror)* from the date for receipt of offers specified above, to furnish any or all items upon which prices are offered at the price set opposite each item, delivered at the designated point(s), within the time specified in the schedule.

| 13. DISCOUNT FOR PROMPT PAYMENT *(See Section I, Clause No. 52-232-8)* ▶ | 10 CALENDAR DAYS % | 20 CALENDAR DAYS % | 30 CALENDAR DAYS % | CALENDAR DAYS % |
|---|---|---|---|---|

| 14. ACKNOWLEDGMENT OF AMENDMENTS *(The offeror acknowledges receipt of amendments to the SOLICITATION for offerors and related documents numbered and dated:* | AMENDMENT NO. | DATE | AMENDMENT NO. | DATE |
|---|---|---|---|---|
| | | | | |

15A. NAME AND ADDRESS OF OFFEROR | CODE | FACILITY

16. NAME AND TITLE OF PERSON AUTHORIZED TO SIGN OFFER *(Type or print)*

15B. TELEPHONE NO. *(Include area code)* | 15C. ☐ CHECK IF REMITTANCE ADDRESS IS DIFFERENT FROM ABOVE - ENTER SUCH ADDRESS IN SCHEDULE | 17. SIGNATURE | 18. OFFER DATE

**AWARD** *(To be completed by Government)*

19. ACCEPTED AS TO ITEMS NUMBERED | 20. AMOUNT | 21. ACCOUNTING AND APPROPRIATION

22. AUTHORITY FOR USING OTHER THAN FULL AND OPEN COMPETITION:
☐ 10 U.S.C. 2304(c)( ) ☐ 41 U.S.C. 253(c)( )

23. SUBMIT INVOICES TO ADDRESS SHOWN IN *(4 copies unless otherwise specified)* ▶ ITEM

24. ADMINISTERED BY *(If other than Item 7)* CODE

25. PAYMENT WILL BE MADE BY CODE

26. NAME OF CONTRACTING OFFICER *(Type or print)*

27. UNITED STATES OF AMERICA *(Signature of Contracting Officer)*

28. AWARD DATE

IMPORTANT — Award will be made on this Form, or on Standard Form 26, or by other authorized official written notice.

NSN 7540-01-152-8064
PREVIOUS EDITION NOT USABLE

33-133

STANDARD FORM 33 (REV. 4-85)
Prescribed by GSA
FAR (48 CFR) 53.214(c)

GPO : 1985 0 - 469-793

**Figure 3-1.** Solicitation, Offer and Award (Standard Form 33).

tory headings. But, since as often as not the headings can appear ambiguous when you first see them, we'll explain each in some detail.

**Administrative Section.** The top eight blocks provide essentially administrative information. Data entered in these blocks will help all concerned to track the bid and contract: who to send it to, the due date, etc.

Block 1 tells whether the contract is a rated order. The government may give certain orders ratings depending on how badly and how soon the order is needed. If speedy completion of a contract is deemed important for national defense, the President can order it handled first over all other contracts. For instance, during the Persian Gulf War some military goods, such as spare parts for Patriot missiles, may have been priority rated by the Defense Department.

There are two levels of priority ratings: DO and DX. DO priority orders have equal priority with each other, but take preference over unrated orders. DX priority orders have equal priority with each other and take preference over DO rated and unrated orders.

If you are working on a rated order, you can impose upon your suppliers to ship you the parts you need immediately rather than at their convenience. A rating, essentially, lets you throw your weight around so you can fill the order on time.

To the right of Block 1 is a block that will tell you how many pages the solicitation contains. This is very important. Count the pages and see that you received all of them. If you find a discrepancy write or contact the person identified in Block 10.

Block 2 is set aside for the contract number. For now this block should be blank. Once the contract is awarded a number will be entered here.

Block 3 contains the solicitation number for the bid document. This is the number you're going to be referring to throughout this offer.

Block 4 identifies the type of solicitation, either a sealed bid (IFB) or a negotiated bid (RFP). (These two procurement processes were explained in Chapter 2.)

The issue date of the solicitation is entered in Block 5. This is the date that the solicitation should have become available to the public, either through a CBD notice or mailing to bidders.

Block 6 is for the requisition/purchase number and should be blank at this time.

Block 7 identifies the government agency issuing the solicitation by name and address.

Block 8 tells you where to send your offer. This block will be blank if you are supposed to send the bid to the government agency that issued the request.

**Solicitation Section.** Blocks 9 through 11 are the Solicitation part of SF33. This tells you more of the nitty-gritty of how to respond to this solicitation request.

Block 9, for example, will tell you how many copies of the offer must be submitted and where and when to submit the offer. Pay close attention. Everything has to be followed to the letter. Disregard the due date given in the CBD. This is the new, extremely official due date and it must be adhered to, down to the hour.

Block 10 identifies a point of contact for information about the bid document. It should include a specific person's name and phone number. In other words, this is someone you can call if you have questions.

Block 11 is a table of contents for the bid document. See that all the page numbers match up with their respective items. Report any discrepancies to the individual in Block 10. You should check this list against your inventory of the bid documents.

The table of contents also identifies which sections of the uniform contract format (see Chapter 4) are being used in this particular document.

Pay particular attention to any mention of Section J attachments. If there is a notation, you should look for a list of attachments included in the bid document, such as drawings and statements of work.

**Offer Section.** Blocks 12 through 18 must be completed in full by the offeror, you. These blocks include the minimum bid acceptance period, discount for prompt payment, acknowledgement of amendments, and administrative information for your company. Give the government as long as you think they need to accept or reject your bid, subject to the standard minimum of 60 calendar days or other provisions if they are invoked. Whether and how much discount you will give for prompt payment is your decision, but may well affect your chances of winning the award. Block 14 is a space for you to acknowledge receiving any amendments to the original solicitation.

Blocks 17 and 18 are extremely important to you. If you do not sign and date the form in these blocks, your offer will not be considered. Period.

**Award Section.** Blocks 19 through 27 contain administrative information that will be filled in by the government at the time of award. This information includes the amount of award, where to submit invoices, who will be administering the contract, who will be making payment, and the name and signature of the contracting officer binding the government to this contract.

## Other Documents You Will Need

As you begin to look over the bid document you will notice numerous references to regulations, specifications, standards, etc. that are not in your bid documents. While these requirements may not be provided but only referenced, you should take care to review them because they will become a part of the awarded contract either in full or in part. These regulations, specifications, and standards contain specific information vital to your bid; they should not be overlooked, as the consequences could mean financial disaster.

How? Let's say a specification calls for a product to be assembled using stainless steel hardware. The specification is referenced but not included in detail in the bid document. You overlook this and submit a winning bid planning to use some other, less expensive type of hardware. You, not the government, will have to change. And guess who will have to absorb the difference in cost? You again. Pay attention to detail.

You should obtain all referenced documents, in whole or in part, and closely examine all requirements listed in the bid documents.

### Federal Acquisition Regulations

One of the pluses of government contracting is that you almost always know where you stand with the government. Unlike private industry, with its free-for-all atmosphere, government contracting takes place in a world where the lines are very clearly drawn. No matter what you are selling or doing for the government, there is bound to be a rule describing how you are to do it or, at the least, how it is to be purchased by the government. Before you can profit from the level playing field these rules give you, you have to understand them.

All agencies of the federal government use a set of rules for contracting and procurement called the Federal Acquisition Regulations (FAR), part of the Code of Federal Regulations. As you page through bid documents, you will find references to FARs, Defense Acquisition Regulations (DAR), and DoD FAR Supplements, depending on who the buying agency is. These regulations describe the responsibilities, liabilities, and rights of the contractor and the buying agency. They should be thoroughly reviewed and understood prior to making an offer.

That does not mean you have to obtain, read, and memorize the entire elephantine regulation book. But you do have to notice when a bid document refers to a FAR. Then you have to look it up, or obtain a copy of the referenced regulation, and see exactly what it says.

Many FARs deal with topics that are not likely to come up in your business—prohibitions against kickbacks, gratuities, and the like. But there could be a FAR in there that says whether you're going to get progress payments or be paid the whole amount upon, and only upon, completion. There may be an explanation of what happens if the government terminates the contract for convenience.

Let's say you develop a patentable invention during the process of fulfilling your government contract. Certain FARs describe whether and how you or the government will get the rights to a potentially valuable patent.

Obviously, FARs can be vital to your chances of making a profit on any contract you land and you need to understand them. FARs are *not* negotiable. If you don't think you can live with a FAR referenced in a solicitation, the best advice is to either petition the contracting officer with a good reason for its removal or not bid the job.

Not all FARs are printed in the bid document, but they are referenced. This is a paperwork reduction effort on the part of the government; but, as pointed out, failing to research the FAR could wind up being a profit reduction for you. You should know how to easily recognize a reference to a FAR and where to find these regulations.

**FAR Numbering System.** FARs usually will appear in the bid document in a listing along with its title. A FAR number might look like this, 11.123-45. The FAR numbering system identifies the part (numbers to the right of the decimal point), any subpart (a one- or two-digit number to the right of the decimal point), the section (a two-digit number to the right of the subpart number and to the left of the dash), and subsection (the number to the right of the dash).

You usually find a preceding paragraph that says:

> This solicitation and contract incorporates the following clauses by reference, with the same force and effect as if they were given in full text. Upon request, the Contracting Officer will make their full text available.

**How to Obtain FARs.** You may get copies of specific FARs in full from the contracting officer. You may also obtain copies of the FARs referenced in the solicitation through a document service or the GPO. The contracting officer is obligated to provide only reference documents that affect the procurement. If you wish to obtain a complete set of FARs you may purchase them from the Superintendent of Documents, U.S. Government Printing Office, Washington, D.C. 20402. However, if you don't ever read anything but the FARs that are referenced, you will be okay. A solicitation should reference every relevant FAR. (See Figure 3-2 for an example of a Federal Acquisition Regulation.)

## Federal Specifications

FARs describe the administrative side of government contract awards. There is a whole different set of rules called Federal Specifications that describe the actual products and services the government buys on a continuing basis.

If you are selling paper clips, lawn maintenance services, or any of a myriad of other goods, you'll become familiar with the Federal Specifications. These specifications define the physical and/or performance technical requirements of goods and services to potential suppliers. They may describe the viscosity of oil, the chemical composition of paint, etc. Federal Specifications are issued by the General Services Administration and are mandatory for use by all federal agencies.

You are in the presence of a Federal Specifications reference when you spot an alphanumeric designation with one to three alpha characters followed by a dash, another alpha character, a dash and a series of numeric characters. For example: ABC-D-123.

The government may also use Commercial Item Descriptions (CIDs) which describe physical and/or performance characteristics of commercially available products. The government may reference a product by its maker and model number, such as Acme Model 1000 Yard Blower and Vacuum. You may be asked to provide that product or its equivalent. The government often simply requests a product with identical specifications to some commercially available item.

## Military Specifications

Items and services procured by the Department of Defense are described in Military Specifications (Mil-Spec). Military specifications give specific requirements to a potential bidder on everything from inspection requirements for precision-machined tools to design and performance requirements for a soft-serve ice cream machine. It is crucial for you to understand the numbering system and composition of a Mil-Spec for one big reason, namely, most government purchases are made by the DoD and have to conform to a Mil-Spec.

ler General does not require original documentation of transportation costs (exclusive of travel).

[48 FR 42187, Sept. 19, 1983, as amended at 50 FR 1739, Jan. 11, 1985; 50 FR 52429, Dec. 23, 1985]

**15.106-2 Audit—Negotiation clause.**

(a) This subsection implements 10 U.S.C. 2313(a), 41 U.S.C. 254(b), and 10 U.S.C. 2306(f).

(b) The contracting officer shall, when contracting by negotiation, insert the clause at 52.215-2, Audit—Negotiation, in solicitations and contracts, unless the acquisition is a small purchase under part 13. In facilities contracts, the contracting officer shall use the clause with its Alternate I.

## Subparts 15.2—15.3 [Reserved]

## Subpart 15.4—Solicitation and Receipt of Proposals and Quotations

**15.400 Scope of subpart.**

This subpart prescribes policies and procedures for (a) preparing and issuing requests for proposals (RFP's) and requests for quotations (RFQ's) and (b) receiving proposals and quotations.

**15.401 Applicability.**

This subpart applies to solicitations issued when contracting by negotiation, except—

(a) Small purchases (see part 13); and

(b) Two-step sealed bidding (see subpart 14.5).

[48 FR 42187, Sept. 19, 1983, as amended at 50 FR 1739, Jan. 11, 1985; 50 FR 52429, Dec. 23, 1985]

**15.402 General.**

(a) Requests for proposals (RFP's) or requests for quotations (RFQ's) are used in negotiated acquisitions to communicate Government requirements to prospective contractors and to solicit proposals or quotations from them. Except as permitted by paragraph (f) below, contracting officers shall issue written solicitations. Solicitations shall contain the information necessary to enable prospective contractors to prepare proposals or quotations properly. Solicitation provisions and contract clauses may be incorporated into solicitations and contracts by reference, when authorized by subpart 52.1.

(b) Contracting officers shall furnish identical information concerning a proposed acquisition to all prospective contractors. Government personnel shall not provide the advantage of advance knowledge concerning a future solicitation to any prospective contractor (but see 5.404, 15.404, and 15.405).

(c) Except for solicitations for information or planning purposes (see subparagraph (e)(1) below and 15.405), contracting officers shall solicit proposals or quotations only when there is a definite intention to award a contract. Subpart 7.3 provides additional instructions for solicitations involving cost comparisons between Government and contractor performance.

(d) A proposal received in response to an RFP is an offer that can be accepted by the Government to create a binding contract, either following negotiations or, when authorized by 15.610, without discussion. Contracting officers should normally issue RFP's when they consider it reasonable to expect prospective contractors to respond with offers, even though they anticipate negotiations after receipt of offers. An RFP shall not be used for a solicitation for information or planning purposes. Solicitations involving cost comparisons between Government and contractor performance (see 7.302(b)) are not for information or planning purposes.

(e) A quotation received in response to an RFQ is not an offer and cannot be accepted by the Government to create a binding contract. It is informational in character. An RFQ may be used when the Government does not intend to award a contract on the basis of the solicitation but wishes to obtain price, delivery, or other market information for planning purposes (see 15.405).

(f) Oral solicitations are authorized for perishable subsistence. An oral solicitation may also be used when processing a written solicitation would delay the acquisition of supplies or services to the detriment of the Government. Use of an oral solicitation



**Figure 3-2.** A page from the Federal Acquisition Regulations.

Mil-Spec numbers use a three-part system. They begin with the designation *MIL* or *DoD* (note that DoD specifications use the metric system of measurement). Some of the older specifications begin with *JAN* representing Joint Army Navy, but these specifications are being phased out and replaced with MIL and DoD.

The next part of the Mil-Spec number will be an alpha character set off by a dash on either side. This alpha letter is the first letter of the first word in the specification. The final part of the number is a series of numbers which have no meaning other than a serial assignment given by the government for that particular specification.

Thus a Mil-Spec number would look something like this: MIL-A-1234 or DoD-D-4567. Mil-Specs are revised from time to time and when this occurs an alpha character will follow the specification number such as MIL-A-1234A.

**Understanding a Military Specification.** Naturally, there is a military specification that specifies what a military specification should look like. The composition of a military specification is defined by MIL-STD-490, Military Standard Specification Practices. This particular instance of military rule making is a benefit to you because it provides for uniformity of format and style so that the reader of any specification will know where to find specific information. Military specifications have six sections and may have appendixes if needed to explain something like special packaging or other uncommon requirements.

Section 1 is titled *Scope* and contains two subsections, *Scope* and *Classification*. The Scope subsection gives a brief general description of the item, material, or process covered by the specification. The Classification subsection describes different categories of an item, material, or process when the specification covers more than one.

Section 2 is titled *Applicable Documents* and also has two subsections, *Government Documents* and *Non-Government Documents*. Under Government Documents you will find a listing of all federal and military specifications and standards and publications which apply to the goods or services being specified. The Non-Government Documents subsection will have a list of relevant specifications and standards from agencies outside the government. Here you are likely to find references to standards set by the American National Standards Institute or the Society of Automotive Engineers.

Section 3 is titled *Requirements* and contains numerous subsections which define, as far as practical, everything required to make the item, material, or process acceptable. Among these subsections you will find requirements for the following:

- *Performance characteristics.* General and detailed requirements for the performance of you and your product or service.
- *Physical characteristics.* Weight and dimensional limits.
- *Reliability.* Requirements of product reliability stated in terms of a numerical goal such as mean time between failures.
- *Maintainability.* Requirements for product maintainability stated in terms of a numerical goal such as mean time to repair.
- *Transportability.* Any special requirements for transportability and material handling.
- *Design and construction.* Any design standards, selection of materials, etc.
- *Workmanship.* The standard of workmanship quality the product must meet to be acceptable.
- *Logistics.* Any special human factors, safety, personnel, training, and supply support requirements. Some of these factors may have subsections of their own.
- *Qualification.* Any testing, validation, or verification that may be required to assess the acceptability of an item.

Section 4 is titled *Quality Assurance Provisions* and contains all the examination, inspection, and testing requirements that are required to verify that the product material or process will meet the requirements in Sections 3 and 5.

Section 5 is titled *Preparation for Delivery,* and contains subsections telling you in detail about preparation, preservation and packaging, packing, and marking for shipment.

Section 6 is the *Notes* section and contains a grab bag of reference information. There are notes to tell you about a product's intended use, definitions of terms used in the specification, ordering data, etc. Appendixes and indexes that are necessary to further explain previous sections may be included at the end of the specification.

## Military and Commercial Standards

The difference between a standard and a specification is this: Specifications provide clear and accurate descriptions of products or services. Standards describe technical and engineering limitations to which those products or services may have to conform.

For instance, you may be asked to install specified electrical equipment in accordance with standards contained in the Uniform Electrical Code issued by the National Fire Protection Association. Or you may be asked to provide engines that use oil of a certain standard.

The idea behind standards is to ensure the quality, uniformity, and interchangeability of the goods and services the government buys. You need to know that, in most cases, when the government references specifications and standards, it is referring to the latest edition. Make sure you have the most recent version of the specification or standard.

You can spot a Military Standard by its prefix MIL-STD and numerical suffix such as MIL-STD-123. It looks a lot like a military specification.

Commercial standards do essentially the same thing as a military standard only they are written by some nongovernment agency such as the American National Standards Institute (ANSI) or the Society of Automotive Engineers (SAE). An example of a commercial standard is ANSI Y.14, which deals with drawing practices.

## Purchase Descriptions and Statements of Work

Two other types of documents that may be found in the bid document are Purchase Descriptions and Statements of Work. When a specification for a good or service is nonexistent, the government may develop a purchase description. The purchase description should identify the physical and functional characteristics to meet the government's minimum needs for the good or service being purchased. You could consider a purchase description the same thing as a substitute specification.

A Statement of Work is just what it sounds like. It will tell you in detail how the government wants a particular task performed. You might find a statement of work on the conduct of new equipment training that will tell you how training materials are to be developed, who will use them, where and when you will conduct classes, and how many students will attend.

## Data Item Descriptions

Data item descriptions, commonly referred to (and pronounced) as DIDs, are another critical part of the bidding and procurement process. Simply, a DID tells you to prepare a document, and how to prepare it.

Generally, this document is going to be some type of report on the product or service you're providing. If you need to give the government a contractor's monthly progress report, a DID tells you how to prepare it. Have to provide a reliability program plan? The DID tells you how.

Chances are the goods or services you will be bidding on will not have any data requirements at all. But if they do, you will certainly want to familiarize yourself with the DID before you do any bidding.

Because government buying agencies are free to pick and choose data requirements as they please, and their desires are all over the map, it's important to understand the DID. Sometimes there may be a requirement for a simple monthly progress report that may take only two hours a month to prepare and can be done with clerical support. Or, there may be a requirement for a logistics support analysis of a product, a big and complex project that eats up thousands of hours and requires the expertise of trained logisticians.

A misunderstood data requirement can make the difference between a contract that returns a profit to you and one that gives you a loss. Therefore, any data requirement in a bid document should not be taken lightly. Investigate data requirements thoroughly until you understand what the contracting agency wants.

**Understanding the DID.** Instructions for preparing the data item description are themselves presented on DD Form 1664 (see Figure 3-3). It provides you with the content, format, instructions for preparation, and intended use of the document to be delivered to the government. DD Form 1664 has 10 blocks.

Block 1 contains the title of the data item description.

Block 2 identifies the agency for which the DID was prepared and gives you its unique DID number.

Block 3 goes into the purpose of the description. This is to give you a general understanding of the data item, its nature, and its use.

Block 4 is the date when the government agency approved the DID for use.

Block 5 lists the office at the agency that is primarily responsible for the DID.

Block 6 will contain an X when a DID requires a scientific or technical report as a product of a research, development, or test and evaluation effort.

Block 7 is used to provide information in the selection and application of the DID in relationship to the specific program or other DIDs.

Block 8 will contain any approval limitations on the data developed by the DID.

| DATA ITEM DESCRIPTION | 2. IDENTIFICATION NO(S) | |
|---|---|---|
| | AGENCY | NUMBER |
| 1. TITLE<br>DATA ITEM DESCRIPTION, DD FORM 1664, PREPARATION INSTRUCTIONS FOR | NAVY | DI-A-2173 |

3. DESCRIPTION/PURPOSE

3.1 A data item description (DID) provides the content, preparation instructions, format and intended use of a data item to be prepared and delivered to the Government.

4. APPROVAL DATE
31 May '77

5. OFFICE OF PRIMARY RESPONSIBILITY
SE (AS, SA, TD)

6. DDC REQUIRED

8. APPROVAL LIMITATION

7. APPLICATION/INTERRELATIONSHIP

7.1 This DID is applicable whenever a contractor is required to develop or revise data item descriptions in support of such documents as specifications, standards, etc.

7.2 This data item description supersedes UDI-A-23345B.

9. REFERENCES *(Mandatory as cited in block 10)*

MIL-STD-100B CH 2<br>
15 APR 76<br>
Handbook H6-1 JUL 74<br>
ASPR 4-113<br>
DoD 5000.19

MCSL NUMBER(S)

10. PREPARATION INSTRUCTIONS

10.1 Unless otherwise stated in the solicitation, the effective date of the document(s) cited in this block shall be that listed in the issue of the DoD Index of Specifications and Standards (DoDISS) and the supplements thereto specified in the solicitation and will form a part of this Data Item Description to the extent defined within.

10.2 Data Item Description (DID), (DD Form 1664).

10.2.1 First Page and Additional Pages. The first page of each DID shall be prepared on the DD Form 1664. If additional space is required, a plain sheet of 8" x 10-1/2" paper shall be used for each additional page. Additional pages including figures, if any, shall be consecutively numbered in the lower right corner for odd number pages and lower left corner for even number pages and identified with the DID number in upper left corner. DIDs shall not contain attachments, appendices, or enclosures.

10.2.2 Block 1 - TITLE. The DID title shall provide a meaningful name for the data item, one which identifies its nature and distinguishes it from other DIDs. It shall be as short as practicable. The DID title shall consist of a basic name followed by such modifiers as are necessary for distinction and ready identification of the nature of the data item. The general procedures specified in MIL-STD-100B for drawing titles shall be followed. The complete DID title shall be typed in upper case.

DD FORM 1 JUN 68 1664 S/N-0102-019-4000 PLATE NO. 19448 PAGE 1 OF 4 PAGES

**Figure 3-3.** Instructions for preparing a data item description (DD Form 1664).

Block 9 lists any other reference documents that may be needed to prepare the data required by the DID.

Block 10 contains the detailed preparation instructions for the data being developed.

### Contract Data Requirements Lists

The Contract Data Requirements List, or CDRL (pronounced "sea-drill") as it is commonly referred to, provides specific instructions for data to be generated as a part of the contract. As you may have guessed, the government has a standard form for this, DD Form 1423, which is illustrated in Figure 3-4. This form tells you what plan or report is required, what DID, specification, or standard to use, how many drafts or submissions are to be prepared, when they are due, and who they are to be distributed to. DD Form 1423 contains 28 blocks.

Blocks 1 through 16 contain information specific to the performance of the CDRL.

Blocks 17 and 18 are for negotiating and preparing the contract.

Blocks A through J are for government administrative purposes. Various codes are entered in these blocks and the government often includes an explanation of the codes with the bid document. However, it would be best for you to obtain a copy of DID DI-A-23434, which will explain these codes.

For our purposes here, be concerned with the description, (Blocks 2 and 3), method of inspection and acceptance (Block 7), method of approval (Block 8), frequency of submission (Block 10), distribution and addresses and number of copies (Blocks 14 and 15), and specific instructions in the remarks block (Block 16).

## Where to Find Specifications, Standards, and Data Item Descriptions

Once you have become familiar with the government's system of specifications, standards, and data item descriptions, it is time to begin building your personal library. Having these documents on hand when you need them can easily make the difference between handing in an intelligent bid by the deadline or not.

Unfortunately there is no hot line you can call to get the specific number of the document you need to build your portable hydraulic-

**CONTRACT DATA REQUIREMENTS LIST**
*(1 Data Item)*

*Form Approved*
*OMB No. 0704-0188*

Public reporting burden for this collection of information is estimated to average 110 hours per response, including the time for reviewing instructions, searching existing data sources, gathering and maintaining the data needed, and completing and reviewing the collection of information. Send comments regarding this burden estimate or any other aspect of this collection of information, including suggestions for reducing this burden, to Department of Defense, Washington Headquarters Services, Directorate for Information Operations and Reports, 1215 Jefferson Davis Highway, Suite 1204, Arlington, VA 22202-4302, and to the Office of Management and Budget, Paperwork Reduction Project (0704-0188), Washington, DC 20503. Please DO NOT RETURN your form to either of these addresses. Send completed form to the Government Issuing Contracting Officer for the Contract/PR No. listed in Block E.

A. CONTRACT LINE ITEM NO.
B. EXHIBIT
C. CATEGORY: TDP ____ TM ____ OTHER ____

D. SYSTEM/ITEM
E. CONTRACT/PR NO.
F. CONTRACTOR

1. DATA ITEM NO.
2. TITLE OF DATA ITEM
3. SUBTITLE
4. AUTHORITY *(Data Acquisition Document No.)*
5. CONTRACT REFERENCE
6. REQUIRING OFFICE
7. DD 250 REQ
8. APP CODE
9. DIST STATEMENT REQUIRED
10. FREQUENCY
11. AS OF DATE
12. DATE OF FIRST SUBMISSION
13. DATE OF SUBSEQUENT SUBMISSION
14. DISTRIBUTION

| a. ADDRESSEE | b. COPIES | | |
|---|---|---|---|
| | Draft | Final | |
| | | Reg | Repro |
| 15. TOTAL → | | | |

16. REMARKS

17. PRICE GROUP
18. ESTIMATED TOTAL PRICE

G. PREPARED BY
H. DATE
I. APPROVED BY
J. DATE

DD Form 1423-1, JUN 90 — *Previous editions are obsolete* — Page ____ of ____ Pages
1007/183

**Figure 3-4.** Contract Data Requirements List (DD Form 1423-1).

actuated cow-milking machine in compliance with government requirements. The government does, however, make available indexes to its specifications, standards, and data item descriptions. These are the *Index of Federal Specifications and Standards and Commercial Item Descriptions, Department of Defense Index of Specifications and Standards,* and the *Acquisition Management Systems and Data Requirements Control List* (AMSDL) DOD 5000.19-L Volume II.

All the indexes are self-explanatory and contain listings of documents alphabetically, by title or by key word, and numerically. You can write to the Superintendent of Documents, U.S. Government Printing Office, Washington, D.C. 20402 to subscribe to these indexes.

If you plan to be doing a lot of government bidding, at some point you probably will want a set of these indexes. That way, if you're in the middle of checking out a bid and you wonder if there's a spec, you will be able to look it up immediately.

When you are getting started, however, you can usually get copies of specifications, standards, and data item descriptions from the government at no cost as long as you do not request more than one copy. To get copies of these documents write to the Commanding Officer, Naval Publications and Forms Center, 5801 Tabor Avenue, Philadelphia, Pa. 19120.

You must provide the name and address of your company, the document number and its title in your request. When you receive your documents, you will find a copy of DD Form 1425, Specifications and Standards Requisition, to use for future requests. You will also be assigned a customer identification number to use for future requests.

Specifications and standards that are developed by nongovernment organizations are not available through the government. That includes widely quoted specifications like those from the American National Standards Institute, so this is something you'll run up against fairly quickly. You can get these documents from the specific organization for a price, often at a discount to members. (See Sources for Additional Information at the end of the text for a list of these agencies.)

Another, and in many ways much preferable source for some of these documents, is your local library. If the public library does not have these on file there may be a science library or university library that has them. If you are in need of only a few documents and the library has them, you may find it much cheaper and faster to go there and run copies than to purchase an entire set and wait for them through the mail.

Finally, there are document service companies which will sell you copies of specifications and standards both public and private. These companies can provide you with copies as rapidly as overnight, but be prepared to pay for services rendered. Fees may be $5 or higher per page. To locate these firms, check the *Business Directory* at your local library.

## Rewards of Careful Bidding

One final point about understanding bid packages. It may sound like a phenomenal hassle looking up all these regulations and specifications and trying to take them into account in your bid. You may be thinking that it's almost certain you will overlook something, with possibly fatal results.

Actually, that is not the case at all. Government contracting regulations and rules deal with complex subjects, so they are not simple. But they are generally clearly written and there is somebody whose job it is to explain it if you do not understand.

You probably will not feel comfortable bidding on the first solicitation you read. But read it, and others. After a time, you will become familiar with the form and details of bid solicitations. You will recognize certain FARs and specifications and how they would impact your bid. When you make a bid, you will do it knowledgeably.

You should understand that the regulations are there for your protection as well as the government's. Before you have been doing contracting very long, you will be able to cite numerous times a government purchaser has told you that you failed to do something you were required to, only to have to eat his or her words when you show documentation proving you did exactly what you contracted for.

When that happens, it's an opportunity for you to offer to do it the government's way—the way the government wants it now—in exchange for more time, more leeway, or more profit. The door does swing both ways.

# 4
# Making Sense of a Bid Document

## How the Bid Document Is Structured

To this point, government contracting may resemble little more than an exercise in reading and filling out endless forms. Nothing could be further from the truth. Successful federal contracting depends on the full spectrum of business skills, from financial management to human resources. The ability to fill out the myriad forms correctly is, however, essential to this arena. Without it, you have little prospect of even getting a chance to succeed as a government supplier.

With that in mind, reviewing the bid document may be the most important factor in determining whether you prosper as a federal supplier. This document is chock-full of text and references that—and this is crucial—will become a legal contract for the successful bidder. I offer this advice as it came to me: "Read the document, set it aside, read it again, set it aside, and read it again."

The legalese in a bid document can often be overwhelming and too much to consume at one reading. By reading the document, setting it aside to let it percolate and then coming back to it, you will better understand what it takes to win and perform the contract.

### Uniform Contract Format

There is, of course, a set of rules in the Federal Acquisition Regulations governing preparation of bid documents. IFBs, RFPs, and RFQs are

| Section | Title |
|---|---|
| | **Uniform Contract Format** |
| | *Part I—The Schedule* |
| A | Solicitation/Contract Form |
| B | Supplies or Services and Price/Costs |
| C | Description/Specifications/Statement of Work |
| D | Packaging and Marking |
| E | Inspection and Acceptance |
| F | Deliveries or Performance |
| G | Contract Administration Data |
| H | Special Contract Requirements |
| | *Part II—Contract Clauses* |
| I | Contract Clauses |
| | *Part III—List of Documents, Exhibits, and Other Attachments* |
| J | List of Attachments |
| | *Part IV—Representations and Instructions* |
| K | Representations, Certifications, and Other Statements of Offerors or Quoters |
| L | Instructions, Conditions, and Notices to Offerors or Quoters |
| M | Evaluation Factors for Award |

**Figure 4-1.** The Uniform Contract Code, as stipulated in the Federal Acquisition Regulations, governs the structure of most bids.

structured according to the Uniform Contract Format, or UCF, defined in FAR 15.406-1. (See Figure 4-1.) Note that the government does *not* have to use this format for the following types of acquisitions:

1. Construction
2. Shipbuilding, ship overhaul, and ship repair

3. Subsistence items (food and other basic bulk commodities)
4. Supplies or services that require special contract forms
5. Firm-fixed price or fixed-price with economic price adjustment acquisitions that use the simplified contract format

For acquisitions other than the ones listed above there are two Federal Acquisitions Regulations, FARs 48 CFR 14.201-1 and 48 CFR 15.406-1, that detail the UCF. There is little difference between the two FARs, and for this chapter we will use 48 CFR 15.406-1, specifically intended for RFPs and RFQs.

**Part I—The Schedule.** The bid document is divided into four parts containing a total of 13 sections. Part I, the Schedule, has 8 sections.

*Section A, Solicitation/Contract Form.* This is the form we mentioned in Chapter 3. This form may be the SF33, SF18, or SF1447. Unlike most sections we will discuss, this form requires information from you. You must complete Blocks 12 through 18 (Figure 3-1) before submitting your offer. Two other sections besides Section A also always require you to provide information. These are Sections B and K. You should carefully review all other sections as they may require your input as well.

*Section B, Supplies or Services and Prices/Costs.* This section, will contain brief descriptions of the goods or services the government wants to buy. It will also briefly describe any supplemental matters such as testing, reports, technical data, and training. Optional Form 336 (See Figure 4-2) is commonly used for listing supplies and services although some bid documents may supply this in a narrative form. Regardless of how it is presented, it should clearly state the description, quantity, and unit of measure of the goods or services being purchased. It should also contain an area for you to enter the unit of measure price and the total amount per item. Later in this chapter we will take a closer look at Section B.

*Section C, Description/Specifications/Work Statement.* This is where you will find a more detailed description of the items identified in Section B. This section may refer to drawings, specifications, and statements of work included elsewhere in the document. It may also identify required sources of supply for components.

*Section D, Packaging and Marking.* This section provides any packaging, packing, preservation, and marking requirements.

*Section E, Inspection and Acceptance.* This section will detail any quality assurance program or requirements.

| CONTINUATION SHEET | Reference No. of Document Being Continued DAAK01-92-B-0080 | | | Page 6 of 84 | |
|---|---|---|---|---|---|
| Name of Offeror or Contractor | | | | | |
| ITEM NO | SUPPLIES/SERVICES | QUANTITY | UNIT | UNIT PRICE | AMOUNT |
| | (End of narrative A004) | | | | |
| 0001 | | | | | |
| | SECTION B - Supplies/Services/Prices<br>SECURITY CLASS: UNCLASSIFIED<br><br>NSN: 3510-01-197-6742<br>NOUN: LAUNDRY UNIT, TRLR MTD, M876<br>FSCM: 81349<br>SECURITY CLASS: UNCLASSIFIED<br>PART NR: MIL-L-44142A | | | | |
| | (End of narrative B001) | | | | |
| 0001AA | PRODUCTION QUANTITY<br><br>ESTIMATED QUANTITY: 95 | AS REQUIRED | EA | $______________ | $XXXXXXXXXXXXXXX |
| | SECTION C - Description/Specifications<br>IN ACCORDANCE WITH MIL-L-44142A with Amendment 1, 14 Aug 90; ECP 91HE6053; & ECP 91HE6068<br><br>SECTION: D - Packaging & Marking<br>PACKAGING/PACKING SPECIFICATIONS: MIL-L-44142A with Amendment 1, 14 Aug 90; ECP 91HE6053 & ECP 91HE6068<br>LEVEL PROTECTION: A LEVEL PACK: A<br><br>SECTION E - Inspection & Acceptance<br>INSPECTION: ORIGIN ACCEPTANCE: ORIGIN<br><br>SECTION F - Deliveries or Performance<br>SEE SECTION F.1, TIME OF DELIVERY<br><br>FOB POINT: ORIGIN<br><br>SHIPPING ADDRESS TO BE SPECIFIED ON DELIVERY ORDER | | | | |
| | (End of narrative B002) | | | | |

NSN 7540-01-152-8067 50336-101 OPTIONAL FORM 336(4-86) Sponsored by GSA FAR (48 CFR) 53.110

**Figure 4-2.** Optional Form 336 used to list supplies, services, and prices.

*Section F, Deliveries or Performance.* This section will list the delivery schedule for goods and services by item, quantity, and time.

*Section G, Contract Administration Data.* This section includes any contract administration data or instructions and any accounting and appropriation data not included on the solicitation form in Section A.

*Section H, Special Contract Requirements.* This section lists the details of any contract provisions specific to this purchase.

**Part II—Section I, Contract Clauses.** This is where you will find a listing of FARs the law requires to be a part of the purchase agreement. You may also find some FARs printed in their entirety if they require information from the bidder.

**Part III—List of Documents, Exhibits, and Other Attachments.** This section provides a listing by title, date, and number of pages for all attachments to the bid document.

**Part IV—Representations and Instructions.** There are three sections in this part.

*Section K.* Here you must provide information on your business and how you comply with applicable laws and regulations.

*Section L.* This details any instructions, conditions, and notices on how to prepare and submit your offer.

*Section M.* This section identifies all the evaluation factors on which the government will base the contract award.

## What to Look For

Now that we have the basics of bid document construction, we can take a closer look at each section. This will help you to know what to look for and understand how parts of some sections relate to others.

### Administrative

Two notable parts of Section A are the type of solicitation and procurement information. This will tell you, for example, whether the bid is unrestricted or there is a small business set-aside. Either one of these can powerfully affect your chances of winning the bid. Section A also describes the government agency that is looking to buy, names your point of contact for more information, gives the due date for your submission, and lists a table of contents. This section may also contain extra information on protests, ordering periods, estimated quantities, and costing instructions.

## The Order Form

Section B is basically the government's ordering form. Anything the government intends to buy and have delivered should show up here. Figure 4-3 is a close-up look at a sample order. At the top of the "Item No." column should be the number assigned to the first good or service to be purchased. This is commonly referred to as a CLIN, for Contract Line Item Number. CLINs are four numbers long and may have subitems designated by alpha characters. In the example, CLIN 0001 is a requirement for a soft-serve ice cream machine in accordance with specification MIL-I-43705D. CLIN 0001 consists of SUBCLIN 0001AA, the production quantity of 100 units.

CLIN 0002 orders data to support the production quantity of 100 units. CLIN 0002 consists of SUBCLIN 0002AA, a technical manual

CONTINUATION SHEET | REFERENCE NO. OF DOCUMENT BEING CONTINUED | PAGE OF

NAME OF OFFEROR OR CONTRACTOR

| ITEM NO. | SUPPLIES/SERVICES | QUANTITY | UNIT | UNIT PRICE | AMOUNT |
|---|---|---|---|---|---|
| | SECTION B-Supplies/Services/Prices | | | | |
| 0001 | NSN: 4110-01-010-0013<br>NOUN: ICE CREAM AND SHAKE MAKER, SOFT SERVE<br>PART NR: MIL-I-43705D | | | | |
| 0001AA | PRODUCTION QUANTITY | 100 | EA | | |
| 0002 | DATA FOR ITEM 0001AA | | | | |
| 0002AA | TECHNICAL MANUAL in accordance with DD Form 1423, contract data requirements list A001 | 1 | LOT | | |
| 0002AB | TRAINING in accordance with Attachment "A" Statement of Work | 1 | LOT | | |

**Figure 4-3.** A sample government order (Section B— Supplies/Services/Prices).

(quantity of one lot), and SUBCLIN 0002AB, training for the equipment. Furthermore, SUBCLIN 0002AA tells you to look at DD Form 1423, CDRL A001, to find the specific instructions for preparing the technical manual. And if you look at the CDRL, you will most likely be referenced to a military standard or specification on preparing technical manuals.

This is just a simple example of how the bid document is constructed. Keep in mind that road maps are not provided.

Be sure you understand the requirements and have the correct revision of specifications and standards, and make certain of the quantities as well as how they are to be priced. If you submit a bid the government accepts, you will have to stand by it even if you made a mistake.

The government also makes mistakes and it is your job to catch them. Check Section B against Section F to see if quantities in the delivery schedule match quantities ordered. Be sure that the delivery schedule follows a logical sequence and makes sense. You should not be required to deliver something before the date established for ordering it. If you find a discrepancy, immediately contact the government buyer given in Section A and ask for clarification.

Section B may also tell you whether the funds to pay for your contract actually exist. In other words, the government may be planning to buy this, but not have the money appropriated yet. This is where you find that out. Section B also gives initial or minimum order quantities, how the government intends to award (only one award or multiple awards), and other contingencies. Here is an example of one possible contingency:

> The successful contractor must obtain government approval of all data requirements under this CLIN prior to government acceptance of any end item production quantity. Failure to timely submit acceptable data and any resulting refusal to accept production deliveries are independent reasons which may justify termination of the contract for default.

Clearly, such a contingency may bear heavily on your decision to bid and your capability to deliver. We will discuss considerations like this in a later chapter.

### Statement of Work

Section C often needs to be read especially carefully. It may contain the entire description of the effort required. Or it may refer you to other specifications and standards or a statement of work, or maybe a combination of both. This could detail nearly anything and everything about your product such as how to paint it, what you are responsible for versus what the government is responsible for or where to buy a part. In any case, if you are given specific instructions, your warning antenna should go up. You can be sure it was spelled out for a reason.

### Packaging and Marking

Section D, on packaging and marking, is supposed to ensure that the item being purchased is adequately packaged and marked to prevent deterioration and damage during shipping, handling, and storage. The instructions may be incorporated by reference to Section C or the specification or statement of work. The packaging and marking requirements may vary between CLINs, so you should check Section B to confirm this. Section D may also contain restrictions on your use of certain packaging materials, such as asbestos. Do not make the mistake of considering packaging a peripheral issue. Packaging and marking requirements may exceed the cost of the unit itself. Take care not to underbid these requirements.

### Inspection and Acceptance

Section E, on inspection and acceptance, defines the level of quality the government wants. It will also tell you how the government plans to inspect your work, outline inspection procedures, and define "acceptance." Remember that the government is your customer and wants a quality product that will meet their specifications. As a contractor you are responsible for controlling the quality of your goods and services, whether you manufacture them or buy them. The government is quite likely to ask you to set up and maintain a special inspection system to control your quality. The government may even specify that the quality control system be in place and functioning prior to awarding the contract.

**Quality Requirements.** Depending on the nature and complexity of the product, there are three general categories for Section E contract quality requirements.

In the first, the government relies on you to do the necessary inspection and testing without telling you in detail how to carry this out.

The second category, a little more detailed, requires the contractor to:

1. Provide and maintain an inspection system acceptable to the government
2. Allow the government to make inspections and tests while work is in process
3. Keep and make available to the government complete records of its inspection work

The third category requires higher-level quality requirements and often imposes military specification MIL-I-45208 or MIL-Q-9858. These are usually specified with complex products requiring in-process controls, detailed work instructions, and documentation control. Higher-level quality is likely to be required if the product is one whose failure could injure someone or jeopardize an important mission. Thus the Stealth Fighter is both a complex and critical item which requires the manufacturer to maintain a higher level of quality than the manufacturer of, say, shoe spoons.

**Types of Inspection.** The government may do the inspection at your facilities (source inspection) or at the place where the government receives the product (destination inspection). Source inspection may mean that a government inspector stops by your factory at a regular interval and randomly inspects the product. Or you may have several government inspectors assigned to your firm who work there daily and require you to furnish them with office space. The government may also require your vendors to allow source inspection at their premises. Vendors have been known to refuse to let government inspectors in. Be sure yours will before you bid on a contract that requires vendor source inspection.

The government usually accepts a product at the point of inspection. If the contract calls for source inspection, acceptance takes place when your product clears inspection at your factory. You will get some sort of certificate, such as a receiving/inspection report attesting to the government's acceptance. Source inspection has two distinct advantages. The first is that you can solve any problems right at your own facility, saving the cost of modifying the product out in the field, perhaps at numerous government installations. The second is that government acceptance at source starts the billing process sooner, meaning you get paid much faster.

The method of inspection or the means of acceptance may mean a lot to the daily operations of your firm. If you do not have a government-approved quality system and you win a contract that requires one, you may have to change your method of operation. Inspection requirements can have a major impact on needs for personnel and office space. You may have to make big changes to the way you work, especially concerning documentation and reporting requirements. For instance if you are working on a project that requires source inspection, you may be required to provide office space for government inspectors. This also means that they will be on premise every day during working hours. This can create all sorts of problems when they try to overstep their contractual authority and tell you how to run your business.

One owner of a manufacturing firm was eager to begin bidding government work and wanted help with the start-up effort. After finding he did not have a government-approved quality system, I explained the requirements. Our discussion ended with him thanking me for my time and telling me he would have to think on this subject some more. I don't think he ever did get into government contracting.

## Deliveries and Performance

Section F, on deliveries and performance, basically tells you when you will have to deliver the goods or services. Under FAR 52-212-1, this section should have a time-of-delivery clause, listing the delivery schedule by CLIN and quantity. Along with the government's own demands, there may also be a place for you to insert your own proposed delivery schedule. This comes in handy if you want to propose an acceleration of the government's schedule. Note that if acceleration of delivery isn't a government evaluation factor, you probably should not propose it because it is of no benefit to you. If you do propose to accelerate, be sure you can. The government may like your proposal enough to make an award and hold your feet to the fire to make the schedule you proposed.

A word should be said for proposing a schedule that is slower than the one the government presented in the bid document. That word is *don't*. You are competing against other bidders and it is almost certain that someone will propose to deliver per the requirements whether they can or not. If you cannot make the government's proposed schedule, it is best to pass.

The government expresses delivery schedules in several different ways. Here are a few common ones:

- Days After Contract (DAC), which simply gives you a certain number of days after the contract signing date in which to deliver the good or service.

- Days After Delivery Order Award (DADOA), which means the good or service is purchased by a delivery order and must be delivered in a set number of days after the date the delivery order is issued.
- Delivery contingent upon delivery or approval of some other contractual item or event, such as 30 days after approval of the first article test report.

When the government sets a delivery schedule, it tries to make a realistic assessment of when the good or service is needed, and what it takes to reach that date. You should make the same assessment and be equally realistic, if not downright pessimistic. Let's say your research says you cannot make the delivery date because a supplier of a major component cannot ship to you until one week prior to delivery and it takes two weeks to assemble a unit. You would be foolish to bid the job hoping that things would work themselves out.

Be sure you know what you are up against on the delivery schedule before you bid. This will save you and the government extra time and effort and grief. If you miss the contractual delivery date, the government may agree to an amended date with no problem. Or, they may decide to terminate the contract and may be able to make you pay to have the product produced by someone else.

Protect yourself against confusion by comparing Section F with Section B and any other section or attachment that contains delivery schedule requirements. Be sure they match. If they do not, write to the point of contact on the bid document and explain where the discrepancy is. We will devote more time to this in the next chapter when we discuss delivery schedule conflicts.

There are a few other clauses you may find in Section F. One possibility is something telling you what to do if you have a government delay in the contract or a stop-work order. You may get instructions on shipping weights, dimensions, and destinations here.

## Contract Administration

Section G, on contract administration data, is mostly for government use. You will, however, find some useful information here. This section will contain any accounting and appropriation data. It will identify the contracting office, and the contracting officer or representative. This will help you understand where to go and whom to contact whenever you have a problem with the contract.

## Special Requirements

Section H is reserved for special contract requirements and as such is tailored to the needs of specific goods or services. As a general rule certain clauses will appear in Section H. These clauses are discussed briefly here:

- *Preparation and distribution of DD Form 250, Material Inspection and Receiving Report (MIRR).* This clause tells you how to fill out and distribute DD Form 250, which certifies government acceptance of a product. The DD Form 250 is often your bill to the government. Do it right or don't get paid.
- *Insurance requirements.* The government may require you to carry worker's compensation, employer liability, general liability, automobile liability, or other insurance in set amounts as it pertains to the performance of the contract.
- *Accelerated delivery.* This lets you accelerate delivery, if you want to, beyond what it says in the contract. It may not, however, compel the government to perform any of its obligations, such as inspections contingent on your delivery, at an earlier date.
- *Engineering change proposals.* This clause tells you how to format, prepare, submit, and distribute any proposals to change the product.
- *Government furnished equipment.* This lists anything the government is going to furnish to you so you can complete the contract. Perhaps the government is furnishing the motors for your soft-serve ice cream machine. This is something you thought you would have to buy.
- *Miscellaneous clauses.* This grab bag of clauses may give special direction on testing and approval of, for instance, first production units. It may tell you about parts that are allowed duty-free entry, give requirements for meetings during the design and development phase, or address any number of other subjects.

## Contract Clauses

Section I, on contract clauses, because of the length and nature of its content, occupies all of Part II. Section I is often considered boilerplate material. However, only those who have read all the FAR clauses and thoroughly understand them should make this assumption. This is where the government, in an effort to reduce the size of the bid document, lists all common clauses. Figure 4-4 shows a typical page of clauses in Section I. These listings may exceed one hundred clauses. We

| CONTINUATION SHEET | Reference No. of Document Being Continued | Page |
|---|---|---|
| Name of Offeror or Contractor | | |

PART II - CONTRACT CLAUSES

SECTION I - Contract Clauses

FAR 52.252-2 CLAUSES INCORPORATED BY REFERENCE (JUN 1988)

This contract incorporates one or more clauses by reference, with the same force and effect as if they were given in full text. Upon request, the Contracting Officer will make their full text available.

(END OF CLAUSE)

NOTICE: The following contract clauses pertinent to this section are hereby incorporated by reference:

| | CLAUSE TITLE | REFERENCE | DATE |
|---|---|---|---|
| 1. | DEFINITIONS | FAR 52.202- 1 | (APR 1984) |
| 2. | OFFICIALS NOT TO BENEFIT | FAR 52.203- 1 | (APR 1984) |
| 3. | GRATUITIES | FAR 52.203- 3 | (APR 1984) |
| 4. | COVENANT AGAINST CONTINGENT FEES | FAR 52.203- 5 | (APR 1984) |
| 5. | RESTRICTIONS ON SUBCONTRACTOR SALES TO THE GOVERNMENT | FAR 52.203- 6 | (JUL 1985) |
| 6. | ANTI-KICKBACK PROCEDURES | FAR 52.203- 7 | (OCT 1988) |
| 7. | PRICE OR FEE ADJUSTMENT FOR ILLEGAL OR IMPROPER ACTIVITY | FAR 52.203-10 | (SEP 1990) |
| 8. | LIMITATION ON PAYMENTS TO INFLUENCE CERTAIN FEDERAL TRANSACTIONS | FAR 52.203-12 | (JAN 1990) |
| 9. | REQUIRED SOURCES FOR JEWEL BEARINGS AND RELATED ITEMS | FAR 52.208- 1 | (APR 1984) |
| 10. | PROTECTING THE GOVERNMENT'S INTEREST WHEN SUBCONTRACTING WITH CONTRACTORS DEBARRED, SUSPENDED, OR PROPOSED FOR DEBARMENT | FAR 52.209- 6 | (JUN 1991) |
| 11. | NEW MATERIAL | FAR 52.210- 5 | (APR 1984) |
| 12. | USED OR RECONDITIONED MATERIAL, RESIDUAL INVENTORY, AND FORMER GOVERNMENT SURPLUS PROPERTY | FAR 52.210- 7 | (APR 1984) |
| 13. | DEFENSE PRIORITY AND ALLOCATION REQUIREMENTS | FAR 52.212- 8 | (SEP 1990) |
| 14. | GOVERNMENT DELAY OF WORK | FAR 52.212-15 | (APR 1984) |
| 15. | AUDIT--SEALED BIDDING | FAR 52.214-26 | (APR 1985) |
| 16. | ORDER OF PRECEDENCE - SEALED BIDDING | FAR 52.214-29 | (JAN 1986) |
| 17. | EXAMINATION OF RECORDS BY COMPTROLLER GENERAL | FAR 52.215 1 | (APR 1984) |
| 18. | AUDIT--NEGOTIATION | FAR 52.215- 2 | (DEC 1989) |
| 19. | NOTICE OF TOTAL SMALL BUSINESS SET-ASIDE | FAR 52.219- 6 | (APR 1984) |
| 20. | UTILIZATION OF SMALL BUSINESS CONCERNS AND SMALL DISADVANTAGED BUSINESS CONCERNS | FAR 52.219- 8 | (FEB 1990) |
| 21. | UTILIZATION OF WOMEN-OWNED SMALL BUSINESSES | FAR 52.219-13 | (AUG 1986) |
| 22. | LIMITATIONS ON SUBCONTRACTING | FAR 52.219-14 | (JAN 1991) |
| 23. | UTILIZATION OF LABOR SURPLUS AREA CONCERNS | FAR 52.220- 3 | (APR 1984) |
| 24. | LABOR SURPLUS AREA SUBCONTRACTING PROGRAM | FAR 52.220- 4 | (APR 1984) |
| 25. | NOTICE TO THE GOVERNMENT OF LABOR DISPUTES | FAR 52.222- 1 | (APR 1984) |
| 26. | WALSH-HEALEY PUBLIC CONTRACTS ACT | FAR 52.222-20 | (APR 1984) |
| 27. | EQUAL OPPORTUNITY | FAR 52.222-26 | (APR 1984) |
| 28. | EQUAL OPPORTUNITY PREAWARD CLEARANCE OF SUBCONTRACTS | FAR 52.222-28 | (APR 1984) |
| 29. | AFFIRMATIVE ACTION FOR SPECIAL DISABLED AND VIETNAM ERA VETERANS | FAR 52.222-35 | (APR 1984) |
| 30. | AFFIRMATIVE ACTION FOR HANDICAPPED WORKERS | FAR 52.222-36 | (APR 1984) |
| 31. | EMPLOYMENT REPORTS ON SPECIAL DISABLED VETERANS AND | | |

**Figure 4-4.** Contract clauses in Part II, Section I of the bid document.

could devote an entire book to this section. For now it suffices to say that this is where you will find clauses on antikickback procedures, utilization of small business concerns and small disadvantaged business concerns, equal opportunity, affirmative action, clean air and water, drug free workplace, discounts for prompt payment, buy American act, termination for convenience of the government, bankruptcy, etc. Welcome to the federal bureaucracy!

There may also be clauses in Section I, written in full or partially written, that give you data on time periods for first article testing and approval or tell you how long the government has to order options and warranty information. Some clauses may require your input, so read carefully. For instance, you may find a clause that references a particular FAR, provides certain information, and requires you to fill in the blanks. Thus you have to look up the FAR, read it, and apply the information provided in the Section I clause to complete the statement.

**Progress Payments.** One clause, the progress payments clause, in Section I deserves individual attention. This clause is designed to stimulate competition and help the small business entrepreneur get a fair share of government purchases. It states in part: "Progress payments shall be made to the Contractor when requested as work progresses, but not more frequently than monthly in amounts approved by the Contracting Officer." This pay-as-you-go concept may reward you with up to 95 percent of your cumulative total costs under the contract. Before you pop open the champagne, take a look at FAR (48 CFR 252.232-7007), which governs payments under the progress payments clause. This FAR goes into great detail on how to compute the amount of progress payments; you can rest assured that the government will require detailed accounting procedures and records of your costs and that they will visit periodically to review them.

## List of Documents

Section J (Part III) is also a separate part of the document. Section J is basically a list of documents that are attached to the main bid document and become part of it through reference. It is crucial not to overlook a document referenced here. Be sure you have all the documents referenced in this section and all pages of the documents. Here you will find specifications, statements of work, contract data requirements lists, and other assorted documents that are peculiar to the good or service being purchased.

**Representations and Instructions**

Part IV requires input from the bidder and also requires the utmost attention to detail. The three sections contained in Part IV have to be completed properly and followed to the letter. A mistake here may render all your bid or proposal efforts useless. The government is very specific about what they want to see in your response. If you do not follow their directions, you may be determined "nonresponsive," which is the same as not filing a bid at all.

Section K will provide several clauses which require you to fill in the blanks. The clauses which appear in this section vary depending on the good or product. Some of the more common ones are briefly discussed here:

- *Certificate of Independent Price Determination.* In this clause you certify that you have not and will not confer with any other bidders about pricing and bidding methods which may result in price-fixing or restricted competition.
- *Contingent Fee Representation and Agreement.* This clause requires you to say if you have retained the services of someone who is not a full-time bona fide employee, such as a consultant, to solicit this contract.
- *Certificate of Procurement Integrity.* In this clause you promise that you have not violated the Federal Procurement Policy Act, which protects the government from wrongdoing by the bidder to get a contract.
- *Miscellaneous administrative clauses regarding your business.* You may have to certify your federal tax identification number, what type of business you are (sole proprietorship, partnership, corporation), business ownership (small business, disadvantaged business, woman-owned business), etc.

Section L will give you some specific direction in preparing your bid or proposal. This includes content, format, and submission requirements as well as restrictions on unnecessary or elaborate responses. You will find out more about this in Chapter 7. Section L also has clauses setting the order of precedence between the bid document, attachments, and specifications. Other clauses describe the type of contract the government intends to award, how to file a protest, acknowledgment of amendments, how late submissions are dealt with, requirement for certified pricing data, and so on.

Section M may look very similar to the instructions given in Section L. However, the method of evaluation can give you some specific insight on what the government thinks is important, ranked from most to least. This information is useful in developing your proposal. In the case of IFBs the government is only concerned with getting what they require at the best price. When you review this section be sure you understand government phraseology such as "lowest responsive responsible bidder." If you don't, ask for clarification. Evaluation factors will be discussed in further detail in Chapter 7.

## Who Should Review the Documents

Two heads are better than one when it comes to reviewing bid documents. As you become familiar with bid documents and the various clauses, you may assemble a review team of people from various departments to help you look them over. You may also want to have the document examined by people outside the company, such as your attorney, a government marketing consultant, or a proposal management consultant. Your document review team will vary depending on what this particular contract is intended to procure. For example, if you have never built a soft-serve ice cream machine but have the manufacturing capability, you may want to go outside the company to hire an expert to design it.

The size of your team is also going to depend on the size of your company. If you have them, representatives from executive management, contract administration, engineering, manufacturing, quality assurance, purchasing, human resources, and accounting will be a part of your review team. Document review is a significant, time-consuming chore but, hopefully, will not force you to hire more people at this stage.

When you are deciding who will see the bid papers, keep an open mind. Don't be afraid to look beyond your usual management team. If our ice cream machine requires a special soldering process for electrical leads, the supervisor or employee familiar with that operation may be the best candidate for information about it.

You do not have to show the entire document to everybody on your team. The chart in Figure 4-5 shows who should review which sections of the bid document. These recommendations, which will help to get you started, should be tailored to meet your needs and organizational structure.

A member of executive management should review the entire document, since the decision to bid or not to bid will ultimately rest with top

| Reviewer | Contract Section A | B | C | D | E | F | G | H | I | J | K | L | M |
|---|---|---|---|---|---|---|---|---|---|---|---|---|---|
| Executive Management | X | X | X | X | X | X | X | X | X | X | X | X | X |
| Contract Administration | X | X | | X | X | X | X | X | X | X | X | X | X |
| Engineering | | X | X | X | | X | | X | X | X | | X | X |
| Manufacturing | | X | X | X | X | X | | | | | | X | X |
| Quality Assurance | | X | X | X | X | | | | | | | X | X |
| Purchasing | | X | X | X | | X | | | | | | X | X |
| Human Resources | | X | | | | | | | X | | X | X | X |
| Accounting | | X | | | | X | | | X | | | X | X |

**Section Description**

A = Solicitation/Contract Form
B = Supplies or Services and Prices/Costs
C = Description/Specifications/Statements of Work
D = Packaging and Marking
E = Inspection and Acceptance
F = Deliveries or Performance
G = Contract Administration Data
H = Special Contract Requirements
I = Contract Clauses
J = List of Attachments
K = Representations, Certifications, and Other Statements of Offerors or Quoters
L = Instructions, Conditions, and Notices to Offerors or Quoters
M = Evaluation Factors for Award

**Figure 4-5.** Contract reviewer checklist.

management. If nothing else, top executives need to know the requirements so they can delegate jobs to the rest of the review team.

Contract administration should review most of the document, with the possible exception of Section C and supporting documentation on design requirements. The responsibility for coordination between your company and the government during the bid stage and after contract award should rest with this individual, who should be thoroughly familiar with the requirements.

Engineering should review in particular Section C and supporting documentation on design requirements. Engineers should also look at the packaging and marking requirements in Section D. This department may also have good input on Sections F, H, or I as they relate to design reviews or delivery dates, especially when they predetermine engineering deadlines. Your engineer can tell you whether the design requirements are realistic, and he or she can spotlight potential manufacturing problems.

The manufacturing department should review the supplies and services, description, packaging, inspection, and delivery requirements (Sections B, C, D, E, F). Manufacturing can warn you ahead of time whether the proposal's requirements will mean new capital expenses, more hiring, or conflicts with existing business.

Purchasing needs to know the same sections as manufacturing. Your purchasing agent can point to potential vendors and possible lead times for getting the supplies you will need.

Quality should review Sections C, D, and E to determine their role in production, test, and delivery. Human resources can provide input to the compliance and certification clauses in Sections I and K as well as to resource requirements and availability.

The accounting department needs to be familiar with Sections B, F, and I. Knowing the quantities required, delivery schedule, and any applicable accounting clauses are imperative to costing the bid.

Finally, put Sections B, L, and M on everybody's review list. Section B defines product requirements and quantities, options, and ordering periods, which have a bearing on your response. Sections L and M provide response direction and evaluation criteria respectively. Anyone involved in the actual response to the bid document should be familiar with these sections.

# 5
# Reading Your Customer's Mind

## Sorting Out Exactly What the Government Wants

By now, you are quite likely wondering how in the world you are going to keep all of this paperwork straight. Not to worry. You will find that after you have been through the review process a time or two, things will fall into place. But there are more than papers for you to keep straight. Establishing what the government wants versus what the government is asking for presents the next problem in your quest for government business.

Let's say you have gone through the bid document several times now. You are sure you understand the government requirements. Right? Maybe, maybe not. Remember that your firm is just one half of the team that is planning this acquisition. The bid document you have received is a form of written communication created by human beings. It is therefore subject to error and probably needs clarification.

It's important that you understand how the bid document was put together and by whom. And it's crucial that you know where to look for trouble spots in those documents.

## The Acquisition Team

During the acquisition process, long before you received the official bid document, a team of government employees was assembled to prepare the document. These employees represented various disciplines within the government, including contract administration, engineering, supply support, training, safety, human factors, reliability and maintainability. Each specialist had his or her own requirements and goals for the design, manufacture, and support of the product you are about to bid on. In addition, members from private industry may have been invited to participate in the preparation of the document by reviewing a draft solicitation and providing comments or by attending and participating in a presolicitation conference.

Add it all up, and there are more than enough cooks involved to spoil your broth. But it doesn't have to be that way, and it is your responsibility to see that it isn't. If you are going to bid this product or service for your company, then you must take up the spoon and be the main cook. That does not mean you should look down on the acquisition team or disregard the value of their input. The team has done its best to prepare and present a document that is concise and at the same time provides for competition. However, it should be viewed as a working instrument in the procurement process, one that is subject to interpretation and change.

## Spotting Trouble

The first and most important problem, and one you will find in many bid documents, is the existence of ambiguities and conflicts in the bid document. The best method for preventing misinterpretation by you or another bidder is to spot these fuzzy areas and conflicts as soon as possible. It is a worthy goal—a misinterpretation can easily cause you to lose the bid or spell financial trouble if you win the award.

Often an error is quite obvious (such as a typographical error) and can be detected while reading the bid document. Other times a mistake will not present itself immediately. It may become apparent during your in-depth analysis of the specification. You may turn it up much later, while talking things over with suppliers, or while you are making your preliminary design calculations.

Suggestions for spotting trouble in the contract, the drawings, the specifications, and the data requirements follow. These suggestions will help you discover conflicts as early and easily as possible.

**The Contract.** While each bid document is carefully tailored for the product or service being purchased, conflicts and inconsistencies will slip through. Be sure to do a thorough review in the following areas:

- Always check to see that everything that is a required deliverable has a line item in Section B ordering its delivery and thus providing a means for you to put a cost on it. If there is not a specific line item, then is there one that is being used to order and cost it. For example, there may not be a specific line item for a Safety Analysis Report to be delivered under CDRL A001, but there may be a line item for all data in Attachment A including all the CDRLs that begin with the letter *A*.
- Check to see if the government has imposed work efforts similar to those being ordered as deliverables that may require the addition of a line item. In other words, sometimes they will tell you to do something but they will not order it. For example, your statement of work may require you to perform reliability and maintainability predictions; a reliability predictions report is ordered under a CDRL, but there is no CDRL for a maintainability predictions report. It may be that it was just overlooked when the document was prepared. Or, it may be that the government wants you to perform this work effort but you are not required to deliver any of the results.
- Once you have established what the deliverables are and what line item they are to be costed under, check to see that the quantities are correct throughout all the sections of the bid document. If Section B orders 100 soft-serve ice cream machines, then Section F should have a delivery schedule for 100 machines as well.
- Be sure that the delivery schedule for goods and services corresponds throughout the document. If Section B states you are to begin delivery of production units 360 days after contract award and Section F states you are to begin delivery of production units 30 days after approval of the first article test report, be sure that these dates correspond.
- Review the equipment or service specification to see whether there are ordering requirements in Section 6 that need to be specified in the bid document. If you find any, review the bid document to see that this has been done. You should find these requirements in Section C but they sometimes appear in other sections.

**The Drawings.** If your bid document was accompanied by a set of drawings, review these documents for content and accuracy. At a minimum, you should do the following checks:

- Review the top assembly nomenclature to be sure it matches the item ordered in Section B.

- Review the top assembly parts list to be sure you have all the listed drawings. While you are at it, make sure you have the correct revision.
- Review all the drawings to be sure they are legible.
- Review each drawing to see if parts listed are identified in the drawing field and vice versa.
- Review the notes on all drawings for additional material requirements or special procedures.

**The Specification.** If your bid document includes a specification for goods or services, it needs to be reviewed for content and accuracy. At a minimum, here is what you need to do:

- Be sure you have no missing pages or missing paragraphs. If your text progresses from Paragraph 3.2.1 to Paragraph 3.2.3, find out what happened to 3.2.2.
- Look for revisions or changes to the text that are noticeable by a different type style. Is the change applicable to that paragraph and does it make sense? Is the paragraph numbering above and below the change in the proper sequence?
- Look for discrepancies between the requirements section (Section 3) and the quality assurance section (Section 4). If there is a requirement in the quality assurance section for testing the emergency shutdown, there should be a requirement for an emergency shutdown in the requirements section. If your soft-serve ice cream machine must pass a test to dispense ice cream at the rate of 1 gallon per minute, as detailed in the quality assurance section, and the requirements section states it must be designed to dispense ice cream at the rate of 0.25 gallons per minute, then you have a conflict.
- Sometimes the specification was developed from another specification for a different procurement. In other words, the acquisition team has tried to modify a boilerplate specification to meet its needs. So watch for references to paragraphs which do not exist or for statements regarding a product that is not the one being purchased. For example, if you read a statement that says the *milking* machine must be equipped with an emergency shutdown system and the bid document is for a soft-serve ice cream machine, chances are you are working with boilerplate material. If you find this to be the case, look further for other discrepancies.

- Requirements statements should be specific to the point of being able to identify design requirements or vendors who can supply the part. A statement such as "an emergency shutdown system will be provided" tells you that it is needed but doesn't explain how the acquisition team intended for it to work. Is it actuated electrically or mechanically? It may be that it doesn't matter, but it should be clarified nevertheless. A requirement for a steering wheel to be a minimum of 15 inches in diameter really doesn't identify the design requirement. Is it 15 inches minimum diameter because your arms naturally rest this far apart or because you need this much diameter to provide sufficient force to turn the wheels when you steer? Ask.
- You may be bidding on a piece of equipment that will interface with another piece of equipment. If so, then you need to understand how the interface works and how the equipment will mate if it does.
- When you review the area of the quality assurance section that deals with testing, you may find some requirements could be performed analytically. If this is feasible, you may be able to get approval to change the requirement as a cost savings.

**The Data Requirements.** If your bid document includes contract data requirements lists (see Figure 3-4), you should review these lists for content and accuracy. At a minimum, here is what you need to do:

- Review the DID number in Block 4 to ensure it is the correct one for the data requirement listed in Blocks 2 and 3. If the DID in Block 4 is for a reliability program plan and the description in Blocks 2 and 3 is for a technical manual, something is wrong.
- If the DID number in Block 4 has a revision letter at the end of it, be sure the one you review is the correct revision. If the number has a "/T" at the end of it that means it has been tailored to give specific instructions that should be included with the bid document. Be sure you have the tailored copy.
- Be sure Block 7 contains the proper inspection and acceptance codes. Otherwise, you may have trouble getting paid.
- If Block 8 is blank, that indicates approval of the data item is not required. While this may very well be the case, we would suggest you request clarification to avoid a conflict at a future date.
- Block 10 is extremely important. If one of the following codes appears—ONE/R (one time and revisions), R/ASR (revisions as

required), or ASREQ (as required)—be sure the "revisions" or "as requireds" are specifically defined in Block 16. Preparing a data item on an as-required basis leaves you at the mercy of the reviewing authority. You may be required to prepare this item twice a year or once a week. You need to have some sort of idea for costing purposes.

- Double-check the total in Block 15. You don't want to be bidding 10 copies when the distribution list in Block 14 calls for 20 copies.
- Above all, be sure that the information given in Block 16 is accurate and complete. If you do not understand it, question it. In particular, understand what is required of each submission, when each submission is to occur, and, if the government is to review and approve each submission, how much time do they have to do this.
- If, when reviewing the DID, you find it has ordering requirements, be sure they are on the tailored DID, CDRL, or somewhere in the bid document.

These lists do not cover all the hazy misunderstandings that can crop up in a bid document. You may find other ambiguities when you start doing preliminary design calculations or when you are sourcing components from your suppliers. Asking questions will not alienate you from your prospective customers, and may give you a leg up on competitors who do not check as closely. If you are required to provide 6 square feet of equipment in a housing with 4 square feet of space and your calculations show this to be impossible, chances are nobody else can do it either. This is worth a question to clarify. If you are required to provide a switch that actuates within 0.0002 nanoseconds and no one manufactures such a switch, ask for clarification.

## Getting the Government to Further Define Its Requirements

You know you are likely to have to query the government contact about vague and conflicting information. Now let's take time to analyze why this should be done and the method for doing it.

First of all, be careful, considerate, and courteous. Remember that you are a potential supplier of the good or service being purchased and you need to treat the government point of contact with the same courtesy you would extend to any of your customers. Since this person in all likelihood will be your main communication link throughout the bid process, you would be well advised to start off on the right foot.

The government is very conscious about not giving any competitor an advantage over another, so don't be surprised if the point of contact is quite businesslike and unwilling to discuss anything other than the procurement. Government procurers are generally not as chatty as your private-sector customers may be. Don't take this matter-of-fact response personally.

Any communication about the bid document should be in writing, period. Remember that the government point of contact is probably working on more than one procurement at a time (in fact, I once talked with one woman who was involved in 85 projects) and does not have a memory like an elephant. Addressing your questions and concerns in writing will not only get you a response but you will also create a record of that communication, which may come in handy at a later date. Questions and answers are often amended into the bid document, providing official clarification on points that are vague or in conflict.

## How to Ask Questions

As your review team makes its way through the document, each individual should jot down any questions they may have. Then a meeting should be arranged for the team to review the questions. All questions should be formatted as much as possible in the same way and combined into one list. This list should be sent to the government point of contact (given in Block 10 of SF33) under a cover letter signed by the person you wish to establish as your company's point of contact, usually the contract administrator or an executive officer.

There is some technique to asking these questions. Mainly, it involves wording the question to get the response you desire. The timing of when to ask the question is also important and is discussed in the next section.

Always remember when you ask a question that there are three parties involved—you, the government, and your competition. Your purpose in asking a question is twofold. First of all, you ask the question to get the answer you want. Secondly, you ask to make the other parties (the government and your competition) aware of the need for information.

Your questions should be well thought-out and written in concise language that specifically defines the problem and offers a solution, if you have one in mind. Don't bother asking questions regarding spelling or typographical errors unless you feel they have an impact on the requirements for the good or service being produced or on a contractual obligation. Questions of this type serve only to add to the mountain of paperwork that already exists and to remind someone who will probably be a part of the team reviewing the bid or proposal that you asked a bunch of useless questions. This type of reminder is not needed in the field of competitive procurement.

A good question directs the person reviewing it to that place in the bid document where it is drawn from. For example, don't ask, "Is the emergency shutdown system to be mechanically or electrically actuated?" Instead, preface the question with the location in the document, such as "Reference Statement of Work 123 for Soft-Serve Ice Cream Machine, Paragraph 3.4 titled Emergency Shutdown System." Now comes the part where you ask for the answer. Your question should go on to read, "This paragraph states that an emergency shutdown system shall be provided. Is a mechanically actuated system acceptable?"

## When to Ask Questions

Now let's examine when to ask your questions. Sooner is better when it comes to any question you need answered in order to make a decision whether to bid or not. You may get a good chance very early. Depending on the complexity of the product, there may be a preproposal or bidder's conference where questions can be asked. But your chance won't go on forever. Obviously, at some point in time there has to be a cutoff point for asking questions. However, if you feel your question is justified, ask it at any time. The most that can happen is the government will decline to answer it or refuse to take any more questions.

## Strategy for Questioning

There is a certain degree of strategy involved in asking questions. Your timing is as crucial as a pinch hitter batting in the bottom of the ninth with two outs and the bases loaded. Questions that are important to your decision making should always be asked, the sooner the better. Questions that do not fall into this category need to be assessed as to whether they give away any information regarding the way you plan to fulfill the government's requirements if you win the contract. In other words, don't tip your hand to the competition if you can avoid it. If you have to ask questions that will ultimately provide your competition with information concerning your suppliers, methods and procedures, or anything else that may with reasonable certainty aid them in their bidding efforts, it is best to delay these as long as possible.

On the other hand, there are times when it is to your advantage to ask questions that do one of two things. These are questions that serve to further define requirements where you feel you certainly have the edge over the competition, and questions which lull the competition into a false sense of knowing what you are doing.

An example of the first would be if you knew that the requirements for soldering a printed circuit board were so precise that it could only be done with robotics, which is the method you already use. You may want to ask a question that draws attention to this. Perhaps you would phrase it like this:

> Reference Statement of Work 123, Cockpit Landing Control, Paragraph 3.5 titled Instrumentation Components. The soldering requirements for printed circuit board, part number 123, are too constraining to be performed without the use of robotics. Would the government accept a change proposal to relax the tolerances of ± 0.00001 inches to ± 0.02 inches?

This question can do two things. First, it serves to inform the competition of the strict soldering tolerance. And, if you have done your homework and chosen your question well, the part is of such a critical nature that there is no way the government will relax the tolerances to a point where robotics is not required. Bingo, you have just served notice to your competition that they will need to purchase robotics equipment, which may be a large enough expenditure to prohibit them from bidding.

Giving your competition information that may mislead them into thinking they know what you are doing is nothing more or less than plain, old CIA-style disinformation. Why would you want to do this? The reason is, it may create a sense of overconfidence just big enough to allow your competition to relax. This in turn may cause them to submit a proposal which is less in some way than they normally would submit, giving you an advantage. It also may allow you to gain a price advantage if they think you are going to use a certain component they can beat the price on, when in turn you have discovered a new qualified source (unknown to them) that is cheaper than anyone.

Let's say the government has a requirement for a portable crane that requires a diesel engine to produce a minimum of 250 horsepower. Through your design calculations you have discovered that you can meet this requirement by using a six-cylinder engine equipped with a turbocharger or an eight-cylinder engine without a turbocharger. Your engine vendor has indicated that the price of both engines is comparable but the turbocharger costs $400. You might ask the government a question such as, "If a turbocharged engine is used, what are the requirements for heat shielding the turbocharger?" Upon reading this question, your competition may assume you plan to go with the turbocharged engine when in fact you have no intention of doing so. If they also plan to use a turbocharged engine, you may have just given yourself an advantage of $400 per unit.

Some final advice about the question-and-answer process: Analyze each question for what it means to you. Don't be fooled by someone else who is using the methods discussed in this section.

Also, be persistent and go for facts, not just show. If you ask a question and receive an answer that is still not clear, reword your question and ask it again, or ask for clarification on the answer. Often you will find that the answer to a question generates more questions. The key here is good communication that serves to define what the requirements of the bid document are. This will help minimize future problems and prevent the creation of bad working relationships.

## Preproposal Conference

Sometimes the government will hold a preproposal conference after the solicitation has been issued and prior to submitting offers. Check your solicitation or the cover letter to see if notification of the conference is there. The purpose of the conference is to brief prospective bidders on the procurement and to read questions and answers.

You will be asked to deliver your questions to the government's point of contact on some date prior to the conference. Normally, you may have at least two persons attend the conference: sometimes I attended as part of a group of five or six. In any event, the government will ask you to confirm that you are coming so that they can make plans for the conference. You will need to supply a list of the names of those attending. The government does a good job of having the necessary personnel attend who can answer your questions.

Plan to arrive in enough time to find your way through an unfamiliar part of the city or a military base. Be there shortly before the starting time for the conference as there likely won't be any appealing place to loiter. I once had to stand for one hour outside a building until the designated 9 a.m. sharp starting time. The government thought letting anyone in early would show favoritism or unfair advantage over other competitors.

After everyone signs in, the conference begins with an introduction of government personnel, handled by the contracting officer who chairs the meeting. Next, you may be supplied with a brief history of the acquisition up to this stage, which may explain how the need for the procurement was identified, when the acquisition team began to meet, the date the solicitation was issued, etc.

After this, a list of all the previously submitted questions with answers is passed out for review. This list includes the questions you have posed along with the questions from the competition. Usually, you are given ample time to review the questions and answers.

Next, everyone participates in an open forum round of questioning. Now you have the opportunity to ask questions about the answers you just reviewed, or to ask any new questions you might have thought of. The government may attempt to answer these new questions immediately or may defer them until later.

The contracting officer will or should make you aware that nothing said or handed out at this meeting is to be construed as new direction for the solicitation. When and only when you receive an amendment to the solicitation, incorporating the minutes of the preproposal conference, do these questions and answers become an official part of the bid document. This is important.

By now, you have figured out that preproposal conferences are not all that glamorous. They do, however, give you a chance to meet the members of the government acquisition team and have a personal talk with them. Preproposal meetings also provide you with your first glimpse of your competition, although you will most likely know this beforehand.

Because you have all these important people together in one place, it pays to put on your psychologist's cap and observe what makes them tick. In particular, watch for your rivals' reactions to the answers the government has provided. You may find a clue you have been looking for, such as how serious company X is about bidding.

### Consultants

Another visitor to the preproposal conference is the consultant. This may be a self-employed individual or a representative of a company. A consultant is there to seek out potential clients to work with on this specific procurement. Sometimes this is not all bad. Sitting out there in the audience with you just may be the foremost authority on the product being procured, who may have even guided the government in the acquisition planning. There is no reason, beyond the inevitable cost, why you should not recruit this valuable person for your own team.

## Amendments to the Bid Document

An official instrument, called an amendment to the bid document, is required to make any changes between the time the document was issued and the last day you can submit bids. This document should be the way you officially receive answers to your questions. In the process, your questions and the answers become part of the bid document—a matter of vital importance.

The government uses Standard Form 30 (see Figure 5-1) for issuing an amendment to a solicitation or modifications to a contract. When you receive an SF30 amendment, check the following areas.

- Block 2 should contain an amendment number which follows a sequential pattern as amendments are issued. If you receive amendment 0003, be sure you have amendments 0001 and 0002.
- Blocks 9A and 9B will provide the solicitation number and date the amendment was issued. Compare the solicitation number to be sure it corresponds to your bid document number.
- Block 11 will tell you whether the closing date for the bid has or has not been extended as a result of the amendment. The contracting officer has the authority to extend this date if the amendment changes the requirements such that extra time may be needed to prepare your bid.
- Block 14 will describe the contents of the amendment, which is usually included on a continuation sheet.

## Making All the Pieces Add Up to a Whole

We have talked about the many areas of the bid document that specify requirements which you, the supplier, will have to provide in your product or service. When you look at these requirements separately, they may all appear achievable and present few problems from a requirements standpoint. But how do they fit in with the day-to-day operation of your business? And how do they mesh with each other? Do all the pieces of the puzzle add up to a whole that you can put together in the required amount of time?

### The Preliminary Schedule

Putting the government requirements into perspective—getting the big picture—should be the last phase of review before you decide to bid or

**AMENDMENT OF SOLICITATION/MODIFICATION OF CONTRACT**

1. CONTRACT ID CODE — PAGE OF PAGES: 1 | 12

2. AMENDMENT/MODIFICATION NO.: F09603-91-R-46643-0005

3. EFFECTIVE DATE: 92 FEB 03

4. REQUISITION/PURCHASE REQ. NO.: FD2060-91-46643,-01 THRU -03

5. PROJECT NO. (If applicable)

6. ISSUED BY — CODE: FD2060
DEPARTMENT OF THE AIR FORCE
DIRECTORATE OF CONTRACTING/LVKB
WARNER ROBINS AIR LOGISTICS CENTER
ROBINS AIR FORCE BASE, GA 31098-5345

7. ADMINISTERED BY (If other than Item 6) CODE

8. NAME AND ADDRESS OF CONTRACTOR (No., street, county, State and ZIP Code)

CODE — FACILITY CODE

(x) 9A. AMENDMENT OF SOLICITATION NO.: X F09603-91-R-46643

9B. DATED (SEE ITEM 11): 91 SEP 26

10A. MODIFICATION OF CONTRACT/ORDER NO.

10B. DATED (SEE ITEM 13)

**11. THIS ITEM ONLY APPLIES TO AMENDMENTS OF SOLICITATIONS**

[X] The above numbered solicitation is amended as set forth in Item 14. The hour and date specified for receipt of Offers [ ] is extended, [X] is not extended.
Offers must acknowledge receipt of this amendment prior to the hour and date specified in the solicitation or as amended, by one of the following methods:
(a) By completing Items 8 and 15, and returning 1 copies of the amendment; (b) By acknowledging receipt of this amendment on each copy of the offer submitted; or (c) By separate letter or telegram which includes a reference to the solicitation and amendment numbers. FAILURE OF YOUR ACKNOWLEDGMENT TO BE RECEIVED AT THE PLACE DESIGNATED FOR THE RECEIPT OF OFFERS PRIOR TO THE HOUR AND DATE SPECIFIED MAY RESULT IN REJECTION OF YOUR OFFER. If by virtue of this amendment you desire to change an offer already submited, such change may be made by telegram or letter, provided each telegram or letter makes reference to the solicitation and this amendment, and is received prior to the opening hour and date specified.

12. ACCOUNTING AND APPROPRIATION DATA (If required)
IN BASIC

**13. THIS ITEM APPLIES ONLY TO MODIFICATION OF CONTRACTS/ORDERS, IT MODIFIES THE CONTRACT/ORDER NO. AS DESCRIBED IN ITEM 14.**

(x) A. THIS CHANGE ORDER IS ISSUED PURSUANT TO: (Specify authority) THE CHANGES SET FORTH IN ITEM 14 ARE MADE IN THE CONTRACT ORDER NO. IN ITEM 10A.

B. THE ABOVE NUMBERED CONTRACT/ORDER IS MODIFIED TO REFLECT THE ADMINISTRATIVE CHANGES (such as changes in paying office, appropriation date, etc.) SET FORTH IN ITEM 14, PURSUANT TO THE AUTHORITY OF FAR 43.103(b).

C. THIS SUPPLEMENTAL AGREEMENT IS ENTERED INTO PURSUANT TO AUTHORITY OF:

D. OTHER (Specify type of modification and authority)

E. IMPORTANT: Contractor [ ] is not, [ ] is required to sign this document and return ____ copies to the issuing office.

14. DESCRIPTION OF AMENDMENT/MODIFICATION (Organized by UCF section headings, including solicitation/contract subject matter where feasible.)
SEE ATTACHED PAGE(S)

NSN: 1740-00-143-8464YW

Except as provided herein, all terms and conditions of the document referenced in Item 9A or 10A, as heretofore changed, remains unchanged and in full force and effect.

15A. NAME AND TITLE OF SIGNER (Type or print)

16A. NAME AND TITLE OF CONTRACTING OFFICER (Type or print)

15B. CONTRACTOR/OFFEROR
(Signature of person authorized to sign)

15C. DATE SIGNED

16B. UNITED STATES OF AMERICA
BY
(Signature of Contracting Officer)

16C. DATE SIGNED

NSN 7540-01-152-8070
PREVIOUS EDITION UNUSABLE

30-105

STANDARD FORM 30 (REV. 10-83)
PRESCRIBED BY GSA
FAR (48 CFR) 53.243

**Figure 5-1.** Amendment of Solicitation/Modification of Contract (Standard Form 30).

not. To do this, you should develop a preliminary schedule that identifies each task called for by the contract, the task's duration, required delivery date, and any contingencies on other tasks.

Start with the identification of program milestones. These are the major events that take place throughout the execution of the program. Contract award, first article presentation, first article testing and approval, delivery of first production units and subsequent lots, provisioning conference, technical manual validation and verification are all considered milestones in a program. Figure 5-2 illustrates a sample milestone chart.

The next step is to list tasks associated with the accomplishment of each milestone and estimate the time required to accomplish the task. With this information at hand you can begin to develop a program evaluation and review technique (PERT) chart. The PERT chart will help you identify linkages or contingencies among tasks and the critical path for accomplishment.

The critical path method (CPM) will help you decide which actions require your utmost attention to reach the end goal. These actions usually have no allowance for slack time, and slippage of the completion date will have a dramatic impact on the program. There are several good books that explain these techniques, if you are not familiar with them. (See Sources for Additional Information at the end of the book.)

Let's look at how this process works (see Figure 5-3). We have just been contracted to deliver 10 eyewashers to the Occupational Safety and Health Administration (OSHA). The required delivery date is 180 days after contract award in accordance with Sections B and F of the contract. Section E states that a first article test report is due 120 days after contract award. The government has 30 days to approve the report. Once

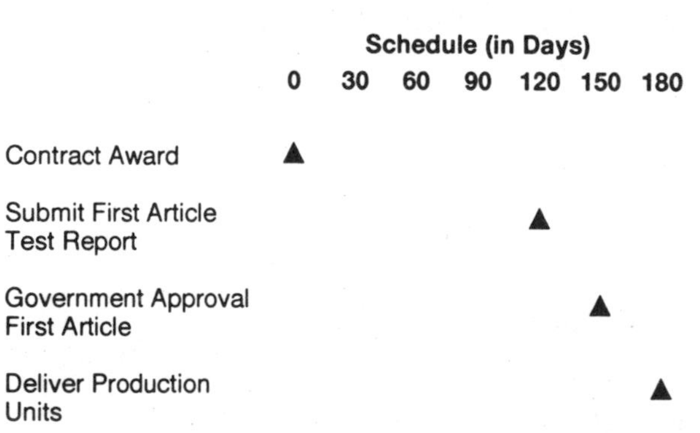


**Figure 5-2.** Milestone chart for the delivery of a product.

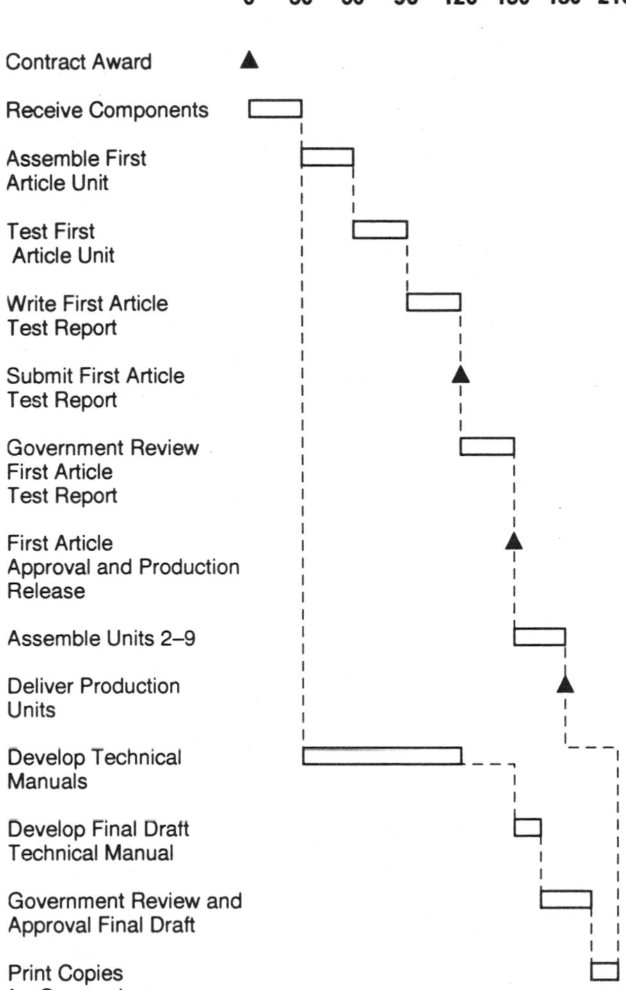


**Figure 5-3.** Production schedule using PERT connections to estimate the time required for each link.

the report is approved, that constitutes approval of the first article unit and releases production of the other nine units. This time frame corresponds with CDRL A001 titled "First Article Test Report." CDRL A002 requires delivery of the final draft technical manual 150 days after contract with government review and approval time of 30 days. The same

CDRL also requires us to pack one copy of the technical manual with each unit. Section B says we must get the technical manuals approved before the government accepts any production articles. Here are our milestones:

1. Ten units have to be delivered within 180 days of contract award.
2. The first article test report is due 120 days after contract award.
3. The government has 30 days to review and approve the test report.
4. The final draft technical manual must be submitted within 150 days of contract award.
5. The government has 30 days to review and approve the technical manual.
6. One copy of the technical manual must be packed with each production unit for government acceptance.

We also know the following from our past experience:

1. It will take 30 days from the date we order to get parts to assemble the eyewasher.
2. Assembly of the eyewasher takes 30 days.
3. We need 30 days to test the unit.
4. We need 30 days to write the test report.
5. We cannot finalize the technical manual until we receive first article approval because changes may be necessary due to test results.
6. It will take 15 days to finalize the manual after first article approval.
7. It will take 15 days from approval of the manual to print the copies needed to pack with the units.

As Figure 5-3 indicates, we have a problem. We will not have technical manuals available in time to pack with the production units for delivery. The government has said they will not accept production units without approval of the associated data items. A closer examination of the scheduling requirements indicates an error on the part of the government. Obviously, the manual cannot be finalized until first article units are approved. If you were to submit final manuals on the very day of approval, the government has still allowed themselves 30 days for review and approval. That means you will not receive notification to proceed with printing until 180 days after contract; the same time production units are required to be delivered.

This example is a simple one. Many contracts will be far more complex. However, you can certainly see from it that every small milestone, task, and detail must be examined and meshed together to obtain the total picture. The problem with the eyewasher contract may be due to the fact that separate schedulers prepared the hardware and software schedules and no one on the acquisitions team went through the exercise we just did. If you discover such a problem, express it in writing to the government along with your reasoning. Chances are they will change the schedule to one that is workable, if still not ideal. At the least, this scheduling effort should help you spot any major milestone problems that may affect your decision to pursue the job or not.

You may want to look into buying some type of program management software that runs on a personal computer. This makes the scheduling effort much easier and also allows you to make changes faster, reduces the chance for error in calculation of time, and lets you enter "what if" scenarios, which you will undoubtedly come across as you develop the schedule. There are a number of good programs that should be available through your local software dealer. (See Sources for Additional Information at the end of the book.)

## Other Sources of Information

There are a few other sources you can go to for help in understanding the bid document.

One source is past history of the procurement. You can write to the government contact and request a copy of the Abstract of Offers from the most recent procurement. This form lists bidders on the last procurement and the amount of their bid by CLIN. It will give you some idea of who your competition is and what a competitive price may be. You can also write for a copy of the solicitation mailing list, which contains names and addresses of firms the government mailed the solicitation to. Some agencies give out the information if you write to them; others may decline and you may have to make your request through the agency's coordinator for the Freedom of Information Act.

If you are the straightforward type who likes to go right to the source, you can call the government contact and simply ask about the past procurement. You may get answers; you may not. You don't know if you don't ask.

Finally, a very good source for information is your own group of suppliers. Suppliers of major components are often working with more than one bidder and can be a wealth of information. For instance, your engine supplier may know what radiator one of your competitors is planning to use.

Asking suppliers for information may be a touchy area and should be approached carefully. It is not out of line to ask a supplier if they are working with another bidder. Asking who that bidder is may be going too far, though. It might be better left for the supplier to volunteer such information. You can find out many valuable details, such as that radiator, while discussing design requirements with the supplier. By keeping your ears open, you may catch a slip of the tongue that can provide you with useful information.

# 6
# To Bid or Not to Bid

## Will It Really Be Profitable?

Our quest to acquire government business has led us to a turning point. We have gathered data, done hours of research, talked extensively with our potential client, and performed a great deal of assessment about just what it is the government wants and what it is we have to do. Now we must ask a question of ourselves: Do we rest and revitalize ourselves for the next leg of the journey, or do we say "Thanks, but no thanks"? Our education in basic business tells us to maximize profits and minimize losses. If we are going to bid, we need to know if there's really a profit to be made.

The first step in determining profitability is learning as much as you can about what it is you have to do and—crucially— how much it will cost to do it. Setting the price depends on a number of variables and merits its own discussion in Chapter 8. Learning as much as you can about what you have to do is another way of saying that you should do a risk assessment. Above all, this requires having accurate and complete information. Other factors play a part in your consideration to bid or not. We will discuss them later in this chapter. But knowing the facts is by far the most important factor in risk assessment.

The members of your review team have performed their fact-finding duties and should now be assembled and given the opportunity to present their findings to the ears of all the other members of the team. This is done to compare notes, allow for objective questioning, and reach a group decision to bid or not. I emphasize the word *group*. Obviously, the people you selected to be a part of the review team will be key players in the performance of this contract should it be awarded. They will have the responsibility to deliver a given quantity at a given time for a set price. If there are any objections to overcome, now is the time to do so before you put the whole company at risk. To determine cost you will have to carefully evaluate each of the following factors:

- Capital expenditures
- Facilities
- Resources
- Overall business plan
- Financing

## Risk Assessment

### Capital Expenditures

What are the costs tied to producing the good or service? If your research says the requirements are within the scope of your normal daily operations, then you are in good shape. However, new capital expenditures need to be looked at from the standpoint of when will they pay for themselves and what is their usefulness beyond this particular project. Remember our example of the robotics requirement for soldering in Chapter 5. If the robotics equipment costs $1 million and the government is only purchasing $500,000 worth of the product, buying the equipment to get the job means you need to have identified another rock-solid market for your soldering services. Things to look for in the area of capital expenditures associated with production or assembly are new tooling requirements, assembly tools or equipment, material handling, process and paint equipment, test equipment, administrative office equipment, etc.

### Facilities

Expansion or structural modification of facilities is a another costly factor. Ask, will my existing production lines handle the assembly of the product? Will existing test facilities accommodate the test requirements? Are door openings, heating and cooling systems, lighting, parts storage areas, and administrative office space the right sizes?

If your facilities are inadequate in any way, you need a detailed plan for expansion or modification and an accurate estimate of the cost involved. Again you need to assess how this fits into your overall business plan. If you have to charge the cost of a new wing to your building to be used for testing this particular product, you may have just costed yourself out of the competition unless all the other bidders are in the same position.

## Resources

Is your existing work force large enough to take on the new project? Do they have the skills necessary to perform the task? If not, are the quantities and skills available within the local area? Relocation expenses should be avoided if at all possible. The cost of training employees is twofold. First, there is the cost of technical training. Second, the cost to bring them up to speed on the job. What is the estimated time span of the learning curve to manufacture, assemble, and test the product? Knowing this will help estimate the number of labor hours per unit. Again you will need to assess how a bigger work force, if necessary, will fit in with your current and future business plans. If you have to hire for the job and then lay off after it, employee orientation and deprocessing are cost factors. Don't forget the costs of wages, benefits, taxes, Social Security, Medicare, and unemployment insurance.

## Business Plan

How does this job fit into your overall business strategy? Will it disrupt any existing projects, and if so, how will you deal with this disruption? Are you going to have to shift personnel from an existing job to the new one? If so, what does that do to the budget of the existing job? It would be nice if the new job fell into the work schedule at precisely the time you were finishing an existing project. However, this seldom happens. Will the new job provide a stable financial base that will allow you to build or expand your business? If so, you need to figure out how long the project will last, how much profit it will generate, and project uses for these revenues in your business plan.

## Financing

The financial status of your company is another element of the risk assessment. Do you have or can you get the necessary credit to perform the project? If you have an established business and a good working relationship with a commercial bank, that may be all you need to obtain credit for a new project, depending on its size. Another source of credit may be an arrangement with your suppliers. Whatever the source, the main concern is that you have arrangements to provide for your needs. To bid a job without knowledge of how to finance it would be disastrous.

The major risk assessment factors in your decision to bid or not to bid are those discussed above. But other elements, although not as important as these, taken as a composite can also contribute to your decision. These elements include the procurement history of the particular good or service and your own or even the government's level of expertise with that good or service.

## What Does History Tell Us?

How often have you heard someone say we learn from our mistakes and from the mistakes of others? This is certainly true in the field of government procurement. The procurement history of a particular good or service can provide valuable insight into your bid decision. It takes some effort on your part to gather the various pieces of information that will collectively provide you with this history, but you will find it time well spent. Again, our goal is to provide the government with a competitive response that meets its needs. Any information that helps you do this may give you an advantage over competitors.

The first thing to do is to contact the government buyer's office and see what information they can provide for you. Below are some questions you may want to ask along with the reasoning for asking them. There are no guarantees you will get specific answers from the government point of contact, but there's nothing to be lost in trying.

1. *When was the last time this good or service was procured?* This will help you to identify things such as advancement in technology, the likelihood of follow-on procurements, and the political and economic climate of the country at that period in time.

For example, if the product was last purchased 20 years ago, it could be that the main reason for a new procurement is to replace outmoded equipment with state-of-the-art technology. If this is the case, and you are responding to an RFP, you probably should place a great deal of emphasis on the technology of your components and manufacturing methods.

If the past procurement history does not indicate any regular pattern, this may have a bearing on your decision to invest in special tooling or equipment to get the job. You might not want to spend too much if follow-on contracts are uncertain.

The political and economic climate of the country during the last procurement may explain any pricing or quantity anomalies. If you are manufacturing a bomb and the last purchase was during a wartime period, that might explain why the previous order was for 100,000 units versus 10,000 units during a peacetime period.

2. *Who was the last successful bidder?* Knowing who won the last procurement can suggest numerous questions that will provide you with a wealth of information.

For example, is this company still in business? If not, did the government contract contribute to its demise and how? You may be able to contact former employees who can provide key information about the last contract. The defunct company may have equipment or resources available to help you if you are successful in acquiring the contract.

Are you in a David and Goliath situation? That is, are you a new company fixing to bid against an established giant in the industry such as Lockheed or McDonnell Douglas? This information will help if you decide to petition the contracting officer to make the procurement a small business set aside. It also may be that the large firm bids the work as the prime contractor and uses smaller firms on a subcontract basis. This may be a niche for your business. Subcontracting can be profitable with a lot less hassle, since the prime has the direct relationship and responsibility to the government.

Has this company been a successful bidder for this product or service numerous times? You may not want to submit a bid just to help the government satisfy their requirement for competitive procurement. Often times bids are what the industry terms *wired,* meaning the bid is technically a competitive process but the odds-on favorite is a successful manufacturer who has won the business numerous times. Also, if this company has performed numerous times in the past then their risk considerations should be less than yours. They should already have the facilities, equipment, resources, business planning, and credit available to do the job.

3. *Was the successful bidder the lowest bid?* Here we are looking for a key to the government evaluation process on the last procurement. Often you will find a clause in the bid document that states the government reserves the right to award the contract to the lowest responsive responsible bidder. At times this is a way out, to let the government avoid a low bidder. If for some reason the government buyer doesn't want to do business with the low bidder, the buyer may declare them nonresponsive and award the business to other than the lowest bid. Funny things happen in the competitive procurement process, but

they're not that hard to understand. You wouldn't want to award a contract to build Stealth fighters to a company who manufactures barbecue grills simply because they knew how to write the proposal and offered the lowest bid, right?

4. *What was the dollar amount of the contract?* The dollar value of the last contract may give you an idea of what the amount should be for the one you are bidding on. However, under no circumstances should you bid blindly based on the past dollar amount, thinking it can be done for that price. The past successful bidder may have bid the job at a loss expecting to make a profit from repeat business. The last contract may have included sizable research and development costs that this one doesn't call for. Remember, bid the job for what you can do the work for. If it doesn't come your way, you're no worse off.

5. *How do current requirements compare to past requirements?* What we are looking for here is some clue to the government's satisfaction or dissatisfaction with the last unit they bought. If the requirements are identical then it's a good bet that they are happy and want more of the same (it may also be an indication they are happy with the last manufacturer and want more of the same). If the requirements from one procurement to the next are notably different, find out why. Perhaps the government in using the product found a need for change. Perhaps the time span between procurements has allowed for newer technology. Whatever the reason, research it, understand it, and emphasize it in your written response if a proposal is required.

6. *Were the goods and services delivered on time in accordance with the contract schedule on the last contract?* Delivery problems stick in the minds of contracting officers who have to answer to their superiors. If there were delivery problems, the source(s) of the problem should be a cause for concern in your bid decision. If delivery was delayed because of a component supplier who happens to be the only source for the component, how will this affect you and what can you do about it? Here is another opportunity to capitalize on an issue when responding to an RFP. Emphasize the fact that you can manufacture and deliver on time, and that you have discussed delivery requirements with your suppliers and they too are committed to the contract schedule. In the eyes of a procurement officer who got raked over the coals when the last contractor performed poorly, promises like these can lead to favorable consideration of your proposal.

7. *How are the units holding up in service?* Again we are looking for the government's satisfaction level with the existing equipment. Are the

existing units reliable? Are they easy to maintain? What about safety and operator-to-equipment interface? These are all growing concerns to the government as they have a direct impact on supportability and ultimately on the life-cycle cost of the equipment.

8. *What is the government buying plan?* The government's fiscal year runs from October 1 through September 30. It is vital for you to understand the realities of government appropriation, allocation, and spending. If money has been appropriated for a fiscal year, it needs to be allocated in that year or the funds may be appropriated elsewhere in the next fiscal year. On the other hand, if funds have not been appropriated, you may be working on a bid that is going nowhere. Another consideration is the date by which the government plans to make an award. Knowing the month tentatively scheduled for award will help you analyze how delivery requirements fit into your business plan.

9. *Where will the product be used?* Environmental conditions under which the product will be used have an impact on the way it is manufactured. These conditions should be spelled out in the specification or statement of work along with any special design requirements. You need to know this for your bid analysis. If you are manufacturing a water cooler to be used by field troops in the desert, it needs more cooling capacity than one for troops in Alaska.

10. *Is there a sample you can see?* If a picture is worth a thousand words, the real thing may be worth immeasurably more. The chance to look at, and take lots of pictures of, existing equipment provides you with a view of your competition. It also provides you with answers to design questions, application of the product, and insight from personnel who use and maintain the equipment. If the government has not scheduled an opportunity to look at existing equipment, request it through the point of contact. If they turn you down, you may be able to find a local company that uses the product, or even visit a military installation to view the product.

11. *Who supplied the major components on the last contract?* Major suppliers on the last contract will most likely be anxious to work with you on the new contract. They may be able to supply goods or services at a cheaper rate than anyone else since they are familiar with the requirements, may already be tooled up to produce, and may be able to add your requirements onto an existing production run. These suppliers are also a good source of information regarding design requirements and problems.

If you cannot get a response to the above questions from the government point of contact, get creative. There are alternate sources for much of this information. For example, you could ask questions of nearly anyone who was involved in the past procurement. This could be former government employees who are now in the consulting field, your suppliers, former employees of past successful contractors, and even your competition.

## Other Influencing Factors

There are a number of other factors that may come into play in your decision whether to bid or not and, hopefully, they will come to light as you study your firm's capabilities to meet the government's requirements. A few more are presented here for your consideration.

1. *Is this your first time for producing this product and/or your first government contract?* If you answer yes to either of these questions, you will need to develop a convincing marketing strategy to be integrated into your proposal. It will need to convincingly explain why you can perform to meet the government's needs better than your competitors can. If your competition has past governmental experience, then they will build this up in their proposal. On the other hand, part of your strength should be your experience in the commercial field with like or similar equipment. If you have never had a government contract, you will need to demonstrate an understanding of the government procurement system and contract administration methods in any case.

2. *Is this the first time the government has purchased this product?* If it is, then they are swimming in unknown waters. Part of your marketing strategy should be geared to comforting the government's uncertainties. This may involve your past experience or expertise in the technology required to manufacture the product.

3. *What effect would your getting this contract have on the local community?* If you are big enough that an increase in your business will increase employment, housing, taxes, and spendable income for your city, you may want to contact local leaders and ask them to help you secure the contract. They may be able to arrange low-cost financing for expansion or equipment. They may also be able to petition your governor, state legislators, or Congressional representatives on your behalf. Isn't that unfair, you ask? It's not your problem. There are laws dealing

with lobbying efforts that your government representatives are aware of. A recommendation or good word of faith on your behalf is not illegal and may help to bring a decision in your favor.

## Are There Hidden Costs?

This question can be answered with two words: "You bet." There are always hidden costs on any contract. Your goal is to try to find them, assess their impact on profitability, and cost them in your bid. Remember, there may not be a CLIN specifically designated for costing every item. You need to determine which is the best one to cost each item under so that you can receive payment as close as possible to the time you make expenditures to accomplish the effort. Most of the hidden costs can be found by a careful review of the bid document and by detailed discussion with the government and your suppliers.

When reviewing the bid document, your routine should be to look for a requirement, find out if the requirement is a deliverable, and then identify what CLIN it is to be costed under. If you find a deliverable that doesn't have a CLIN, ask the government if it was overlooked. If you don't succeed in getting an amendment to add a CLIN, don't assume that means the work is not required. Often the government will impose a work effort in the specification or statement of work and not require it to be delivered. They may, however, visit you and ask to review this work.

### Reviews and Meetings

Search your bid document for any wording about reviews or meetings. The government likes to monitor contractor progress, particularly if you are undertaking a research and development program. The bid document for an R&D program will be chock-full of meetings such as those listed below:

- Preliminary design review
- Critical design review
- Program review
- Guidance conferences for logistics support analysis, provisioning, training, and technical manuals
- In-process reviews for logistics support analysis, provisioning, training, and technical manuals

- First article examination
- Configuration audits
- Maintenance demonstrations

These reviews require a considerable amount of effort on your part to plan and execute. You need to make facilities arrangements, prepare presentation material, set aside time for staff members to attend the review, and follow up on action items generated from the review. Try to get the government to specify how many reviews or meetings will be conducted, how long they will last, where they will be held, and the time schedule for them. Otherwise, you will have trouble costing them, which could mean a sizable reduction in profits. If your bid document states that program reviews will be conducted throughout the life of the contract, does that mean once a year, every quarter, or monthly? Will they last 1 day or 1 week? You see how this can affect the cost of the bid.

### Delays

Another hidden cost is that of delays by the government, a supplier, or your firm. Surely you didn't think that you could undertake a program that has a defined schedule for everything without Murphy's Law coming into play? The unfortunate effect of this is that you cannot anticipate when a delay will occur or what impact it will have. One deterrent to delay is to study the schedule in advance and be sure that it is a workable one. You have to allow time for mailing or shipping, government review, possible rework, etc. If the government is at fault for a delay, the government is usually agreeable to a schedule modification to compensate for the amount of time caused by the delay. If you are at fault for the delay, the government may not be so amiable. A delay in schedule can be cause for termination of the contract. Therefore, be sure you have a firm commitment from your suppliers on delivery dates and quantities and a written understanding of the consequences for a delay. Also be sure that whoever has the responsibility of monitoring your internal schedule has the means of enforcing it with the help of the executive branch, if necessary. Avoid delays at all costs. The government makes a note of any delays and this can have an impact on your future business with them.

Regardless of the source of the delay it will create some unexpected cost in your performance of the contract. Again, if the delay is attributable to the government, then you can negotiate for the cost of the delay.

If the delay is on your part, then you will lose money. While I know of no way to cost for this ahead of time and put it in your bid, you need to be aware that this can and most probably will occur sometime during the execution of the contract.

### Misinterpretation

Differences of interpretation are additional sources for hidden costs. You will find that parts do not function as they are supposed to or your supplier told you they would. You will find that vendor-supplied documentation does not fully meet the government requirements. These are just two examples of inadequacies that will rear their heads throughout the life of the program. When this happens you will need to act swiftly to avoid delay. This may mean concession on your part to maintain the success of the program. Differences of interpretation are going to happen any time two people communicate. This is why we have spent so much time reviewing the bid document and asking for clarification. Hopefully, this effort has eliminated a lot of these differences, but it will not catch them all. When you find you have a difference of interpretation your best choice is to tactfully work on a resolution. It may be less costly to keep an open mind and be willing to resolve the issue than to end up in litigation. This is not to say that you roll over and play dead, accepting the other parties' interpretation when you know you are right. But keep the cost of being right in perspective.

In summary, the decision to bid or not to bid is made with as much accurate and complete information as can be obtained. Your risk assessment, analysis of past procurement history, and knowledge of hidden costs will help you make the decision to either shelve this effort and wait for another or commit the money and resources necessary to succeed as a government contractor. If your decision is positive, the remaining chapters in this book will help you achieve your goal.

# 7
# Preparing a Winning Pitch

First off, congratulations. If you have reached this chapter, you are serious about pursuing a government contract. Now it is time for the next step, and it is a crucial one.

This chapter presents basic guidelines for preparing your proposal. For procurements that require a written response, this is the most important effort you will undertake in becoming a supplier to the government. You can spend hours upon hours researching the requirements and coming to a comprehensive understanding of them. You can spend an equal amount of time pricing components, estimating labor, overhead, capital expenditures, and other costs associated with the performance of the contract. But if you don't spend the time necessary to understand the proposal requirements and communicate how you can perform them, everything else will have been wasted.

## Should You Write Your Proposal In-House or Subcontract the Effort?

The art of proposal writing requires two basic skills! The writer has to be able to effectively communicate your ability to perform the government requirements and, at the same time, provide an underlying theme that sells your company. To accomplish this you need a cross between a technical writer and a marketing expert. You may be that person, or someone on your staff may be that person. There are also numerous consulting firms who specialize in proposal writing. These firms provide professional expertise that is often not available from within your organization. They may be contracted to perform the whole effort or parts of it, as your needs dictate.

## The Five C's of Subcontract Management

Your decision should be based on an evaluation of the factors involved in making a subcontract effort successful. A successful subcontract effort must incorporate the five C's of subcontract management. These are cost, control, content, continuity, and confidentiality.

**Cost.** The cost of writing the proposal must be kept in perspective to the profit derived from getting the contract. Obviously, it would be unwise to spend $100,000 on a proposal for a contract whose net profit is less than that. But proposal costs can mount quickly and easily run into many thousands of dollars whether they are written by in-house personnel or by outside consultants. Here's an example:

If you assigned a team of six people whose average hourly wage is $17 to work full-time for a month, your cost for writing would be $16,320 ($17 × 8 hours × 6 people × 20 days). If you subcontract a team of six people at rates from $37.50 to $125 per hour (which is not uncommon in today's market), your cost for writing would be $36,000 to $120,000. This cost is just for writing and editing. You will also be charged for transportation and per diem if the work is done at your facility. You will incur additional costs for copying, assembling, packaging, and delivery.

This example presents a great case for writing the proposal with in-house staff. You should at least consider taking on a major part of the effort, time allowing, and using the expertise of a consultant for strategy, editing, or review.

**Control.** Controlling the subcontract effort is extremely important. Remember, it is your firm that is making the bid and it is your firm that must respond by the submission date. If you are going to subcontract all or part of the proposal effort, you will need to keep a tight rein on your subcontractors. You can do this by making them a part of the team.

Be sure that you and the subcontractor understand what is to be done, how it is to be accomplished, and when it is to be done. Establish a clear line of administration with someone from your staff functioning as the proposal manager. If the subcontractor wishes to assign a proposal manager that's all right, so long as it is understood that your proposal manager is the one in charge.

The subcontract effort is easiest to control if you can monitor it throughout the day or at least at regular intervals (every two days, weekly, or upon scheduled completion of a section). If the subcontractor is willing to work at your facility and you can afford it, this is the best arrangement. You will then be able to monitor the work effort as well as provide quick responses to questions from the subcontractor. If your arrangement is one that allows the subcontractor to work on the project away from your facility, be sure to establish a procedure to monitor progress. Make sure you see it, not just hear about it. Do not accept progress reports over the telephone. It doesn't cost that much to fax a report or send it by overnight mail. Plus it will help to speed up the review process. In either case, whether the subcontractor works on-site or off the premises, you should plan for regular reviews of the material and the schedule, which both of you participate in.

As with any good business agreement, the what, when, and how should be defined in writing, up front. You can do this with your purchase order. Once you have defined what the subcontractor is responsible for and the time frame for performance, you should request a staffing plan.

The staffing plan should detail the subcontractor's level of effort and resource commitment by position. That is, how many managers, writers, editors, and illustrators will be assigned and how long they'll be assigned to this task. This will cause the subcontractor to think about the job and do some advance planning. It will also help you assess whether your subcontractor agrees with you on the amount of resources required to complete the project on schedule. From this, you should be able to determine how many of your own personnel it will take to support the subcontractor.

**Content.** The content of your proposal will convey to the government review team how you intend to meet the requirements of the bid document and why you are best qualified to do so. How you relate this to your subcontractor will have a bearing on your success as a bidder. This should be much more than a sales pitch, however. Whatever you submit as a part of your proposal, you are going to have to make good on. Be sure your subcontractors understand this and that you provide accurate information for their use.

It is important that the subcontractors understand your facility, manufacturing methods, management philosophy, departmental procedures, and anything else that may be covered in the proposal, to the depth that they can accurately explain it in writing or through an illustration. This means that for the duration of the proposal effort you should consider them as employees and a part of your team.

Remember: Everything written by a subcontractor must be reviewed by someone within your organization who has the knowledge and authority to commit to what is being said.

**Continuity.** The fourth element in subcontract management is continuity. To obtain it, maintain a group of personnel that are committed to the job from start to finish. The last thing you want to happen is to have personnel assigned to a 90-day program move on to another program in 60 days, forcing you to send someone else in to finish the job. This could spell disaster for your proposal effort. Be sure that the subcontractor guarantees people will be assigned to the job for the duration. Then, barring any of the usual events in life that cause disruption, you should have a solid team to work with. Most subcontractors will not have any problem in agreeing to do this. It is to their benefit as well as yours. After all, if they do a good job for you, you may have other business for them.

**Confidentiality.** A final word about using a subcontractor. While most subcontractors are honest and discreet, it is a good idea to have them enter into a confidentiality agreement. This agreement should strictly prohibit them from divulging any information regarding the proposal or your company methods and procedures to any person or firm without your express written permission. They should also be limited to working on your proposal only.

Another type of agreement that may enter the picture is a teaming agreement. The teaming agreement usually obligates you, the prime contractor, to use the subcontractor for other work efforts on the particular contract you are bidding. In exchange for this, the subcontractor agrees to not bid their services for these efforts to another prime contractor. In other words, they will help you write a proposal if you will give them the subcontract for preparing the required technical manual or whatever. If you sign such an agreement, be sure that the subcontractor has the ability and financial strength to do the job.

## Choosing Your Proposal Team

The proposal team, much like your review team, should be made up of people who can lend their specific expertise to a written response. The bid document will require discussion on various topics from engineering design to the qualifications of key personnel.

Your department heads or someone on their staff should be well qualified to provide information on these topics. The trouble is, they may not be qualified writers. What's more, they may not be inclined to do this type of work and may need encouragement to get it accomplished. This is where professional help can be of benefit.

Professional proposal consultants can provide total management, or writing, editing, and review services. They can also provide an objective view to the way things should best be presented. Whatever the composition of your proposal team, the following positions and responsibilities should be assigned.

## Proposal Manager

The proposal manager is the administrative head of the project. All communication regarding the proposal should flow through the proposal manager. The responsibilities of the proposal manager are:

- Plan and design the proposal outline and schedule
- Supervise the daily activities of the proposal effort
- Monitor the proposal schedule and report progress, delays, and resolutions to executive management
- Assign staff to write, edit, and review the proposal material
- Ensure that all staff members have the correct documentation (bid document, amendments, standards, specifications) to perform their task
- Participate in any meetings with the government to discuss contract and proposal requirements
- Ensure that the theme of the proposal and key ideas are incorporated in the proposal where applicable

The proposal manager should have a general knowledge of your company's methods and procedures as well as the operation and performance of the product you are bidding on. The proposal manager should most certainly be in command of the English language. Poor grammar and sloppy sentence structure in a proposal are a reflection of how you run your business. Additional qualifications in selecting a proposal manager include an understanding of contracts, the ability to work well under pressure, and good motivational and people skills.

### Proposal Writer

The proposal writer is the person who is tasked with the actual research and writing of proposal text. The extent of the task may range from a subsection to an entire volume. The responsibilities of the proposal writer are:

- Perform research and gather information on the issues they are writing about
- Write text and develop figures and illustrations to enhance or clarify text
- Coordinate the preparation of final figures and illustrations that are to be included in their assigned text
- Monitor the proposal schedule to ensure that submissions are on time
- Notify the proposal manager of any problems with writing assignments and suggest possible resolutions
- Monitor any changes in the bid document and update proposal text as necessary
- Participate in proposal team meetings
- Edit other writers' text as assigned by the proposal manager
- Incorporate the theme of the proposal and key ideas into the writing assignment

Proposal writers should have a specific knowledge of the issues they are assigned to write. They should also be well versed in the use of the English language. Additional qualifications include the ability to work well under pressure, creativity, and adaptability.

### Proposal Editor

The proposal editor is responsible for reviewing the proposal text, figures, tables, and illustrations for format consistency, presentation, accuracy, completeness, and compliance to the requirements of the bid document. The responsibilities of the proposal editor are:

- Review text and artwork and mark changes or questions
- Coordinate editorial comments with the writer to be sure there is an understanding of what the change is and why it needs to be made
- Monitor the proposal schedule to ensure that the editorial process is on time

- Notify the proposal manager of any problems and suggest possible resolutions
- Monitor any changes to the bid document and review material for compliance
- Participate in proposal team meetings
- Incorporate the theme of the proposal and key ideas
- Maintain consistency and continuity of writing style among the writers and throughout the proposal material
- Review material generated by the writers to be sure that overlapping information coincides

Proposal editors should have a general-to-specific knowledge of the material they review. They must be extremely familiar with grammar usage and sentence structure. They must be detail-oriented to catch those little mistakes that happen. Proposal editors should be able to maintain an objective viewpoint when editing, which will allow them to ask questions and get answers before the government review team does.

### Clerical Support

Clerical support is the glue that holds the proposal effort together. Not enough can be said about the importance of having someone around who can competently tie all the loose ends together. And, believe it or not, there is always something that is forgotten until the last minute. Among the qualifications you should consider for clerical support personnel are:

- Good grammar
- Detail orientation
- Good personal computer skills
- Good reproduction equipment skills (copying and fax machines)
- Ability to work well with people under pressure
- Initiative to go that extra mile

While the proposal manager, writers, and editors are banging their heads together trying to create the proposal, this person is the one who pulls it all together behind the scenes. We will discuss this in detail further in the chapter.

### How Many People Do You Need?

Now that we have discussed the responsibilities and qualifications for the various proposal team members, I am sure that you are wondering, how many people does it take to write a proposal? The simple answer is that the number of personnel you need depends on what you have to do and how quickly you have to do it.

The best way to determine how many people you need is to develop an outline and a schedule. From this you should be able to make an accurate assessment. Keep in mind that proposal writing can be a full-time job. Therefore, you should plan for other people to pick up some or all of the duties of the personnel assigned to work on the proposal. The outline and schedule will help you define who is capable of writing which sections. It may be that one person is assigned an entire section or only a single subsection.

To keep your staff at a minimum—which will help maintain continuity in the proposal as well as reduce the disruption of your normal operation—look for people who are qualified to write more than one section and also edit other sections. For instance, your engineering manager may be able to write the technical design section as well as the manufacturing section. This person may also be able to edit the quality section.

## Drafting Your Proposal Outline

Section L (Instructions, Conditions and Notices to Offerors or Quoters) and Section M (Evaluation Factors for Award) of the bid document will provide you with the information you need to draft an outline of your proposal. In these sections you will find specific instructions on the content, format, and length of the proposal as well as how it will be evaluated by the government's reviewers.

Aside from a number of administrative paragraphs giving direction on the number of copies to submit, where and whom to submit to, and how the contract will be awarded, you will find specific instructions about the structure of the proposal. Figure 7-1 illustrates these instructions.

The example shown here is a fairly detailed one, but you can see that it identifies the number of volumes, volume title, number of copies required for submission, a cross-reference to the Section M evaluation factors, and a page limitation. Note that page limitations are not always given.

**Figure 7-1.** Structure requirements for a proposal (taken from Section L in the bid document).

The offeror shall submit technical proposals as a package separate from the pricing proposal and other portions of the solicitation. The offeror shall make no reference to price in the technical proposals. The technical proposal shall address only those items identified in paragraph (e) below. Only one technical proposal for each tow tractor (MB-4 & Flight Line) from each offeror shall be considered, representing only one configuration. The offeror's technical proposal and any subsequent changes thereto shall be incorporated in any resultant contract and the commitments made therein shall be binding upon that offeror. In cases of any conflict or ambiguity between any offerors technical proposal (including amendments) and the Government specifications or other Government requirements, the Government specifications shall govern. Offerors are advised to submit technical proposals which are clear and comprehensive without additional explanation or information.

Risks, including cost, schedule, performance and technical are to be identified and addressed in each Volume where applicable. Where risks are identified, approaches for resolving or avoiding the risks should be discussed.

The proposals are to be structured as follows. Offers are to be submitted in the number of copies of the volumes as identified below. The data is to be contained in spiral binders with the exception of Volume III and Volume VII which are to be in standard three ring binders. Standard 8 1/2" × 11" paper shall be used for text. Left, right, top and bottom margins are required to be at least one inch wide. Pica or Elite type is to be used and there are to be no more than 6 lines of type per inch. If proposals are printed front to back, offerors are requested to print them head-to-head. Each volume and copy shall be in a separate binder. If data submitted exceeds the page limitation for that Volume, the excess unread pages will be returned to you. Title pages and table of contents are to be limited to three pages but will not count in the volume page limitation.

| Volume | Title | No. of Copies | Cross-Reference | Page Limitation**** |
|---|---|---|---|---|
| I | Past Performance | 4 | | 15 Pages |
| II | Reliability and Maintainability | 3 | Area I, Item 1 | Section 1: 15 Pages<br>Section 2: 10 Pages |
| III | Engineering* | 7*** | Area I, Item 2, Factors 1, 2 and 3 | 75 Pages |
| IV | Manufacturing** | 4 | Area I, Item 3, Factors 1, 2 and 3 | 45 Pages |
| V | Management | 4 | Area I, Item 4, Factors 1, 2 and 3 | 20 Pages |
| VI | Logistics | 3 | Area I, Item 5, Factors 1 and 2 | 20 Pages |
| VII | Cost Data | 6*** | Area II | No Page Limit |
| VIII | Proposal, Terms and Conditions Subcontracting Plan | 5*** | | No Page Limit |

(*Continued*)

**Figure 7-1.** *(Continued)*

*Volume III, calculations, commercial literature, and drawings shall be included in appendices which are excluded from the page count. Drawings may be placed in a pocket.
**Volume IV, Each diagram/flow chart which is a fold out will count as 1 page. Fold outs shall not exceed four 8 1/2 × 11 inch pages and shall fold entirely within the page size of the binder.
***This number includes the copies as required by L-900, para (b).
****Page Limitations apply to each proposal if multiple proposals are submitted, each must meet the limitations specified above, for each volume.
The contents of each volume shall be as follows. Offerors are cautioned that their technical proposals will be incorporated into the resultant contract and offerors will be bound by their content. Any change in your technical proposal after award shall be executed by an Engineering Change Proposal.

Also given in painstaking detail as a part of your instructions is the method for binding, paper size, type style, margins, and even how many lines per inch. Follow these instructions to the letter. You wouldn't want your proposal considered nonresponsive because you used the wrong size paper or bound it incorrectly. If you feel the need to deviate, write the government contact and request permission.

You may wonder why the government is so specific. The reason is that this helps the government be sure that no one bidder has an advantage over another. In other words, you are all playing on a level field. Also, the government review team will be looking at many proposals. If all proposals are structured the same, it makes their job easier. If the reviewer expects to see an explanation of how your soft-serve ice cream machine operates in Section 3.1, and you have located it in Section 3.4, which is on another page, you may receive a comment stating you did not address this evaluation factor.

The detailed instructions given in Section L provide the skeleton for your proposal outline. From this you should add the sections and subsections for each volume (often these are also supplied in Section L), being sure that you have identified a place to cover all of the evaluation factors given in Section M. If you have page limitations for each volume, you may want to break this down further by section or subsection. The final component of the outline is staff assignments for writing and editing. This should clearly identify by name who is responsible for each section or subsection. Figure 7-2 illustrates a proposal outline developed from the instructions in Figure 7-1.

**Figure 7-2.** Outline for a proposal, with staff assignments.

| Paragraph/Title | Writer | Editor |
|---|---|---|
| **Volume I Part Performance (15 Pages)** | | |
| 1.0 History of Previous Government Contracts | ____ | ____ |
| 1.1 Significant Achievement on Previous | ____ | ____ |
| Government Contracts | ____ | ____ |
| 1.2 Relevant Commercial Experience | ____ | ____ |
| 1.3 Quality Program | ____ | |
| **Volume II Reliability and Maintainability Analysis (15 Pages)** | | |
| 1.0 Reliability Program | ____ | ____ |
| 1.1 Reliability Requirements | ____ | ____ |
| 1.2 Critical Reliability Considerations | ____ | ____ |
| 1.3 Reliability Demonstration Test Schedule | ____ | ____ |
| 1.4 Reliability Deficiency Program | ____ | ____ |
| 1.5 Reliability Program Organization | ____ | ____ |
| 1.6 Reliability in Development | ____ | ____ |
| 1.7 Reliability in Design | ____ | ____ |
| 2.0 Maintainability Program | ____ | ____ |
| 2.1 Maintainability Requirements | ____ | ____ |
| 2.2 Critical Maintainability Considerations | ____ | ____ |
| 2.3 Maintainability Demonstration Test Schedule | ____ | ____ |
| 2.4 Maintainability Deficiency Program | ____ | ____ |
| 2.5 Maintainability Program Organization | ____ | ____ |
| 2.6 Maintainability in Development | ____ | ____ |
| 2.7 Maintainability in Design | ____ | ____ |
| **Volume III Engineering (75 Pages)** | | |
| 1.0 Four Wheel Steering System | ____ | ____ |
| 1.1 Preliminary Build List | ____ | ____ |
| 1.2 Reliability & Maintainability Design Approach | ____ | ____ |
| 2.0 Braking System | ____ | ____ |
| 2.1 Preliminary Build List | ____ | ____ |
| 2.2 Reliability & Maintainability Design Approach | ____ | ____ |
| 3.0 Vehicle Integrity and Design | ____ | ____ |
| 3.1 Chassis | ____ | ____ |
| 3.2 Cab | ____ | ____ |
| 3.3 Conceptual Design Data | ____ | ____ |
| 3.4 Engine and Transmission | ____ | ____ |
| 3.5 Reliability Design Approach | ____ | ____ |
| **Volume IV Manufacturing (45 Pages)** | | |
| 1.0 Facilities/Methods/Equipment and Production Flow | ____ | ____ |
| 1.1 Assembly | ____ | ____ |
| 1.2 Manufacturing Staging | ____ | ____ |
| 1.3 Workstations for Subassembly | ____ | ____ |
| 1.4 Support Facilities | ____ | ____ |
| 1.5 Paint Facilities | ____ | ____ |
| 1.6 Testing Facilities | ____ | ____ |

*(Continued)*

**Figure 7-2.** (*Continued*)

| Paragraph/Title | Writer | Editor |
|---|---|---|
| **Volume IV Manufacturing (*Continued*)** | | |
| 1.7 Storage | ______ | ______ |
| 2.0 Preliminary Schedule | ______ | ______ |
| 3.0 Staffing Plan | ______ | ______ |
| **Volume V Management (20 Pages)** | | |
| 1.0 Organization | ______ | ______ |
| 1.1 Executive & Administrative | ______ | ______ |
| 1.2 Manufacturing | ______ | ______ |
| 1.3 Engineering | ______ | ______ |
| 1.4 Quality | ______ | ______ |
| 1.5 Purchasing & Inventory Control | ______ | ______ |
| 1.6 Resource Allocation | ______ | ______ |
| 1.7 Relationship of Proposal Team to Implementation Effort | ______ | ______ |
| 2.0 Staffing | ______ | ______ |
| 2.1 Key Personnel Résumés | ______ | ______ |
| 2.2 Relationship of Key Personnel to Program | ______ | ______ |
| 2.3 Recruiting and Training Plans | | |
| 3.0 Communication and Control/Risk Management | ______ | ______ |
| 3.1 Preliminary Program Schedule | ______ | ______ |
| 3.2 Approach to Meeting Major Schedule Risks | ______ | ______ |
| 3.3 Management Information System | ______ | ______ |
| 3.4 Inventory Control System | ______ | ______ |
| 3.5 Subcontract Efforts | ______ | ______ |
| 3.6 Prime/Subcontractor Interface | ______ | ______ |
| 3.7 Systems Engineering | ______ | ______ |
| 3.8 Configuration Management System | ______ | ______ |
| **Volume VI Logistics (20 Pages)** | | |
| 1.0 Provisioning | ______ | ______ |
| 1.1 Provisioning Plan | ______ | ______ |
| 1.2 Provisioning Schedule | ______ | ______ |
| 1.3 Engineering Changes and Provisioning | ______ | ______ |
| 1.4 Long Lead Time Items List | ______ | ______ |
| 2.0 Technical Manuals | ______ | ______ |
| 2.1 Technical Manual Plan | ______ | ______ |
| 2.2 Technical Manual Schedule | ______ | ______ |
| 2.3 Validation Procedures | ______ | ______ |
| 2.4 Technical Manual Changes | ______ | ______ |
| **Volume VII Cost Data (No Page Limit)** | | |
| — Cost Figures and Supporting Rationale | ______ | ______ |
| **Volume VIII Proposal, Terms and Conditions, Subcontracting Plan (No Page Limit)** | | |
| — Completed Terms and Conditions from Bid Document | ______ | ______ |
| — Subcontracting Plan | ______ | ______ |
| — Exceptions to Bid Document | ______ | ______ |

## Preparing the Proposal Schedule

The government has a tendency to take as much time as it needs to prepare the bid document, then give you very little time to respond. Therefore, the first thing you should do is assess the amount of time you have to work on the proposal versus the amount of time given by the government to respond. Don't be fooled into thinking that you can respond to a bid document that took months to complete by assembling a team of employees for the weekend locked up in a mountain retreat somewhere.

If you feel the time allotted for preparation and submission is unreasonable or unachievable, write the contracting officer and ask for more time. If you don't ask, you'll never know.

Identify a date to start work on the proposal and a date to finish. The date to finish should be a fair amount of time ahead of the submission date to allow for assembly, packaging, and delivery. With this time frame established you can estimate the amount of time required to complete each section or subsection of the proposal and allocate resources accordingly to allow for writing (you may have time to prepare more than one draft), editing, and reviewing. Figure 7-3 is a milestone chart for the proposal schedule, developed from the outline in Figure 7-2. Note that the figure illustrates only the first three of the eight required volumes.

When developing your proposal schedule, keep these four scheduling guides in mind:

1. Not all sections can be worked on beginning with the start date. Information for some sections such as manufacturing and management are readily available. Information for other sections such as engineering and cost will evolve as you go through the process of preliminary design and sourcing components. You should prepare those sections that you have information for first and get them out of the way so that there will be fewer tasks to complete when you are running short on time.
2. The editing process should start as soon as there is text to be edited. Don't let this effort pile up on you thinking that all it requires is a quick look-over. During the course of editing you may find something that requires an entire rewrite. You don't want to make this discovery at the last minute.
3. Don't overload the schedule for those who have multiple writing or editing assignments. Be sure to allow them enough time to do the job right the first time.

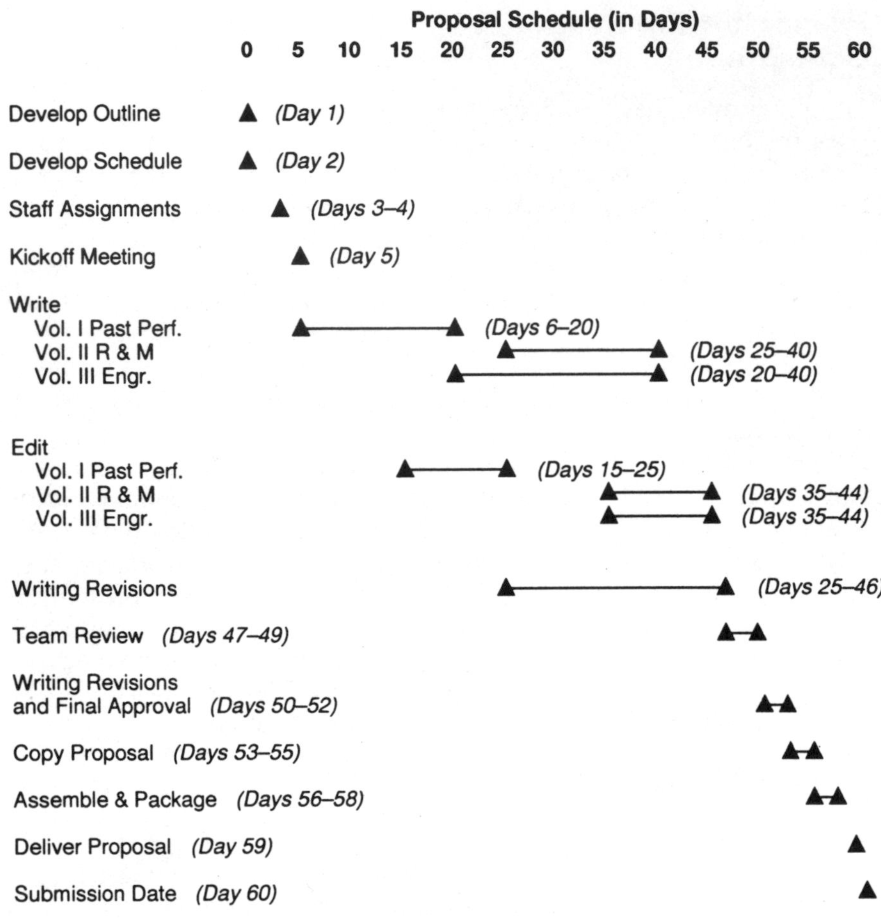


**Figure 7-3.** Milestone chart for the proposal schedule.

4. Allow ample time for the copying and assembling process. You never know when the copying machine is going to break down. It may be best to postpone the copy and assembly process until the end making it easier to remove and insert changes.

## Writing, Editing, and Reviewing the Proposal

Writing, editing, and reviewing the proposal is a subject big enough for its own book. In fact, there are a number of good books already published on this subject, which you can find at your local library. (See Sources for Additional Information at end of book.) This section will get you started with some basic tips on understanding the bid document requirements and on writing, editing, and reviewing the proposal.

## Understanding the Bid Document Requirements

Once again, Section L is loaded with little tidbits like croutons on a salad. If you push them aside, the flavor is not the same and they are still there when you finish. While all of the instructions in Section L are meaningful, some merit our attention more than others. Here are examples of meaningful instructions to look for:

- "Elaborate documentation, expensive binding, detailed art work, or other embellishments are unnecessary." In other words, fancy four-color brochures bound in leather with a promotional fly swatter will get you nowhere. Simple paperboard binders with black and white artwork are perfectly acceptable. This does not mean that you can't use color artwork. Simply use it with discretion.
- "The offeror's proposal for the requirements shall be clear, coherent, legible and prepared in sufficient detail for effective evaluations by the Government."

  Write definitive sentences and don't ramble on. For instance, "An electronic governor rated at 2100 RPM will be mounted on the right side of the engine."
- "Technical proposals shall follow the Purchase Description (PD) format with appropriate responses to each paragraph; identifying offeror's method of compliance, indicating design features and method of construction."

  Writing the proposal in the same order as the purchase description allows the reviewer to march through your material methodically. The task of confirming that you have addressed each design or component requirement is much easier if it follows the order of the PD. Tell the reviewer what they are getting. For instance, "The cylindrical storage tank for the soft-serve mix is constructed of 12-gauge stainless steel."
- "Proposals stating that the offeror understands and will comply with the Statement of Work, or paraphrasing the Statement of Work or parts thereof, are considered inadequate. Phrases such as 'standard

procedures will be employed' and 'all of the technical factors cannot be detailed in advance' are also inadequate."

Again, tell the reviewer what you are going to do and how you are going to do it. If the Statement of Work (SOW) states that "a storage tank will be provided for storing the soft-serve mix," don't respond, "A storage tank will be provided in accordance with Paragraph 1.2 of the SOW." By doing this you haven't told them any more than they told you.

You might reason that they have been ambiguous and so should you. In effect, what they have done is given you a requirement with the latitude to be creative in your design to meet the needs of your manufacturing methods. By telling them "the cylindrical storage tank for the soft-serve mix is constructed of 12-gauge stainless steel," the government now knows that the tank will be round, is made from a material thickness that most likely will withstand puncture, and will not rust or contaminate the soft-serve mix.

- "The offeror's technical proposal and any subsequent negotiated changes thereto shall be incorporated in any resultant contract and the commitments made therein shall be binding upon that offeror."

  The impact of this statement is twofold. First, anything you say can and will be held against you in a court of law. Second, it serves as fair warning that if you offer more than is required, it will be *accepted* and *expected*. Again, the best thing to do is to provide what the government asks for at the best price that you can supply it. That's why you don't see hood ornaments on military jeeps.

## Writing to Win

Writing a proposal is somewhat like giving yourself a performance review. It forces you to analyze your strengths and weaknesses. You then capitalize on your strengths and downplay your weaknesses. Writing to win requires you to maintain a positive style and a continuity to your work.

Maintaining continuity during the proposal effort while using a variety of personnel requires you to develop a theme and key ideas that can be included throughout the various sections of the proposal. The theme should express why you are best qualified to supply the product or service being purchased. It should be supported by key ideas that emphasize your strengths as they are applicable to the requirements.

**Blow Your Horn.** You should make every effort to tell the government how good you are at the things the government wants from you. As we have discussed previously, on-time delivery is very important in government contracting. If your history of meeting or exceeding the delivery schedule of your clients can be documented, by all means, tell the government.

For example, "XYZ Company has manufactured and delivered over 5000 Soft-Serve Ice Cream Machines to over 20 different clients in the past 10 years. All of these machines have been delivered on time in accordance with the client's schedule. Eighty percent have been delivered ahead of schedule."

Provide examples and explain your system for meeting these schedules. If you have experience either directly or indirectly with the product or service being purchased, build this into the text. For example, "XYZ corporation has manufactured the Model 12 Soft-Serve Ice Cream Machine for over 20 years. This model meets or exceeds all requirements of Military Standard MIL-I-1234."

If your methods and procedures are unique or you are using state-of-the-art technology, let the government know. The more they know about you, the better chance you have that they will make a decision in your favor. Just be sure that you don't overdo it to the extent that you lose sight of explaining how you intend to meet the requirements for the product or service.

An executive summary placed at the front of the document is a good place to highlight your strengths, with an emphasis on brevity. Handle the details in your proposal text. The purpose of the executive summary is to give those individuals who will not be reading all of the proposal text a feel for your company and what you can do. Your executive summary should be brief but informative.

**Writing Guide.** A style guide for the writing of the proposal will ensure that sections read alike. Consistency in format is important in making reviewers comfortable when they read your proposal. If your proposal is written in several different styles, it might give the impression that the writers didn't confer with each other during the effort, which could reflect on your business practices. Figure 7-4 is a sample style guide that can be used to get you started. Tailor it to your theme, to your approach to writing, and for whom you are writing.

Beyond maintaining continuity and style there are a number of tips that can be given about proposal writing. Anyone who has ever worked on a proposal can supply you with more of them than you care to listen

**Figure 7-4.** Sample style guide for writing a proposal. [*Richard Watkins*, Style Guide for Proposal Writing in Response to Government Requests for Proposal *(previously unpublished), copyright 1992. Reprinted with permission.*]

## STYLE GUIDE FOR PROPOSAL WRITING IN RESPONSE TO GOVERNMENT REQUESTS FOR PROPOSAL

**Sentence Structure.** Use simple sentences in favor of compound-complex structures.

(*Inappropriate*) Following the completion of the test plan review by the inspector, the selected unit will be released to the company's testing department to begin duration testing, and a notice will be sent to the Quality Control Manager and the on-site government representative, who are then required to monitor the test phase and review the documentation.

(*Better*) The inspector first will review the test plan for the selected unit. If approved, he will release the unit for testing. Notified beforehand, the Quality Control Manager and the on-site government representative will then monitor the test and review the results documentation.

**Transition.** Within paragraphs, connect thoughts logically. Describe anticipated performance results as cause and effect. Detail a product or component structure from most significant to least significant. Outline a procedure in a sequence of steps.

**Level of Detail.** Use as much as needed. Where possible, employ an exhibit.

**Technical Terms.** Commonly understood terms of government procurement are acceptable. Spell out abbreviations at point of first usage, followed by the abbreviated form in parentheses. Terms specific to vendor products or items not commonly dealt with in the industry must be defined at point of first use.

**Reference.** Cite external documentation (contract sections, military standards and specifications, etc.) in specific terms. Do not supply just the standard number (MIL-STD-1585) alone, but include an applicable section or paragraph number (MIL-STD-1585, Section 3.2.1).

Make intraproposal cross-references just as specific as external ones (Technical Proposal, Subsection 1.15.2.3).

The basis for the cross-reference must be clear. Do not assume that the reader has made the connection by just the citation alone.

**Figure 7-4.**

(*Inappropriate*) The configuration plan will be submitted in accordance with the requirements of DOD-STD-480.

(*Better*) The configuration plan will be transmitted on the forms prescribed in Para 4.7.1 of DOD-STD-480.

**Verb Tense and Voice.** Use the *present tense* in syntax describing programs, practices, methods, etc. that are in place or soon to be in place at the company. This might include organizational structures, CDRL procedures, handling configuration changes, preparing Level III drawings, etc. Use the present active in describing the physical and performance characteristics of equipment, product components, etc. that already exist or are known in the industry.

Save the *future active* for programs, practices, procedures, etc. that will be set up as a result of the contract award. This might include training, special review boards, test plans, certain CDRL items not previously provided by the company, etc. Describe product design, if completed during the proposal development phase, in the present active. Use future active to discuss the design work to be done after contract award.

(*Present active*) The Project Engineer reviews the drawings before they are released to the Manufacturing Department.

(*Present active*) The Quality Assurance Division directs the TQM Program.

(*Future active*) The size of the coupling will determine the fuel hose specification.

(*Future active*) If the switch is eliminated, the operator will be able to start the pump in less than 10 seconds.

The use of present active or future active, however, does not preclude the use of past tense forms when appropriate. But it does discourage the use of passive voice constructions regardless of tense; for example, "The Program Manager signs drawing in the approved box" and NOT "The drawing will be signed by the Program Manager in the approved box."

**Numbers.** Spell out values of ten or less except when used with a unit of measurement. (Nine students, three hinges, 2 feet, 180 pounds, 30 gallons per hour, etc.). Write decimals and fractions in numerical (digit) form.

(*Continued*)

**Figure 7-4.** *(Continued)*

**Punctuation and Capitalization.** The conventional rules apply. In addition, consider the following.

1. End sentences that introduce a list, table, or exhibit with a period.
2. End each item description in a list with a period.
3. Capitalize the complete names of the company's organizational components (i.e., Finance Department, Engineering Division) and key personnel titles (Program Manager).

**Format.** Text will appear in a decimal format per the document outline provided. Level of subordination will be limited to a sixth position.

Enumerate items in a list if they are sequential or value-ranked in nature. Bullet items that are nonsequential and equal in importance.

Exhibits are stand-alone items that are keyed to the governing section. Use "Figure 1.3-2" referring to the second figure in section 1.3, as opposed to "Figure 1.3.2-1" referring to a figure belonging to section 1.3.2. Title all exhibits, including tables.

to. Hopefully, the ones you find here will serve to keep you on the right track to success:

- Write at a level that the reader will understand. Your proposal will most likely be reviewed by a subject matter expert. However, don't assume this person to be a genius. If you are introducing a new concept, explain it. The reviewer may not be as "up to speed" on this as you are.
- Take care when using the same information in more than one volume or section. What is old hat to one reviewer may be Greek to another. Terms and buzzwords may need to be explained where introduced so that everyone reading the text will understand.
- Make your sentences informative and concise. Try to limit the length to no more than 20 words. Remember that the reviewer is going to look at several proposals. It is very easy to lose concentration or forget which proposal you read something in. Short informative sentences will stand out in the reader's memory.
- Good grammar is important. If you have questions concerning grammar, there are a number of colleges and universities that can answer these questions for you. To locate one in your area write to Grammar

Hotline Directory, Tidewater Community College Writing Center, 1700 College Crescent, Virginia Beach, VA 23456.

- Try not to cross-reference from one volume to another. The reviewer or reviewers may only have the volume they are responsible for reading. You don't want to make them walk to another building a half mile away to see what you referenced.
- Tables, illustrations, charts, and line drawings help to break the monotony of reading page after page. Be sure these visuals emphasize a point and enforce your text. Don't just throw them in without providing text that explains them. Also try to keep them the same size as your text pages and avoid making the reader have to turn the volume sideways to view them.
- If you are using material that was previously prepared for another project, be sure to review it for changes and applicability. This will avoid confusing the reader, which leads to irritation and bad memories.
- When working with a page limitation, be sure to cover all the requirements, allocating your space for each according to its rank of importance in the evaluation process.
- Think positively and write positively. Do not apologize for any weaknesses you think you have. Remember you are selling your abilities to the government. You must instill in them confidence in your ability to perform.
- Avoid too much hype. Too many adjectives can cloud the issue. It can also leave the reviewer with the impression that you are trying to smooth over something you don't understand.
- Don't assume that the government is familiar with your company or work no matter how good your reputation is. Explain your company history just as if you were talking to a new employee who had never heard of you.

## Editing: a Three-Step Process

Editing the proposal is like icing a cake. You have mixed all the ingredients, put the pan in the oven, and baked a solid object. But somehow until it is iced, it just doesn't look right. It's not finished. The same goes with editing. Your job as an editor is to put the finishing touches on the proposal.

The editing process is best accomplished in increments that have specific objectives rather than by trying to cover all the bases at once. Since it is easier to do this in small parts, I would suggest reviewing a section at a time. This will also provide you with information that can be retained from start to finish.

A common form of editing is to use a three-step process. You read through the material once, editing for grammar, again for accuracy, and finally for how well the material presents itself. I would suggest doing these three steps in the order given so you are not subconsciously remembering a little mistake here and there. This allows you to concentrate on the final product.

The grammar edit is performed to correct sentence structure, spelling, punctuation, and proper use of nouns, adjectives, and verb tense.

The accuracy edit is to confirm any figures, statistics, or statements that may be questionable. Be sure you have identified your source and can document your references just in case the government asks you to.

The presentation edit confirms a number of things. Read through the proposal just to see how it reads. The following list of questions will help you with this final step in your edit.

1. Does text read smoothly or are the sentences choppy?
2. Is there a smooth transition from one subject to another or does text bounce back and forth between ideas?
3. Does text progress through the requirements in the same order as the statement of work or purchase description?
4. Has the theme been carried out throughout the document?
5. Are key ideas expressed in the appropriate places?
6. Does material that has been cross-referenced agree?
7. Have the style and format instructions been followed throughout the document?
8. Do tables and illustrations have supporting text?
9. Are references to tables, illustrations, and other sections or paragraphs correct?
10. Are pages, paragraphs, tables, and illustrations numbered in sequence and are they complete?
11. If you were reviewing the proposal how would you rate it? Are there things left unexplained?

Editorial comments should be specific. If you want something changed, don't leave it to the imagination of the writer. Besides telling the writer what is needed to make the text better, give the reason why it is needed. It may be that you have misinterpreted the thoughts being expressed.

Remember we are talking about communication between two human beings. Keep the line open. Comments concerning grammar, style, and format should be written on the document and returned to the writer for correction. This lets the writer know what is being changed. Be sure to use an ink color different from the text (red is the accepted standard).

### Reviewing the Proposal

Now that you have written and edited the proposal to its winning form it is time to subject it to a good review by qualified experts. Gather your proposal team, lock the doors, and don't accept any phone calls or other interruptions. You may also want to bring in outside consultants. In the proposal business this is known as a "red team review."

The purpose of the review is to give your proposal one last look before the government has its opportunity. You should try as much as possible to review the material objectively. This is why it may be a good idea to invite someone who is not associated with the company on a daily basis to participate.

You are basically looking for the same things discussed in the writing and editing sections of this chapter. The main difference is that you are critiquing the proposal as a team, not as an individual. If the consensus is that you have met the requirements of the bid document, expressed key ideas and carried the theme throughout the entire document, and have beyond any doubt left the reviewer with the knowledge to make a decision that you are the best company for the job, you are ready to submit.

If on the other hand you find things that need revision, assign them to the responsible party for rewrite. Don't subject this individual to a mass rewrite at the meeting. This only leads to discouragement and confusion, which is not what you need at this point in time. Hopefully, the requirement to revise text or figures will be minimal and can be done quickly after the review. It is not necessary to reassemble the team for another review unless the changes are major. Simply assign an editor who understands what needs to be changed.

## Behind the Scenes

There are a number of things that need to be planned for besides the writing, editing, and reviewing of the proposal. While they may seem to be less important, your proposal will not be complete without them.

Therefore, empower a person with outstanding clerical abilities and great organizational skills to carry out the following responsibilities.

### Printing or Copying

You have created a mountain of paperwork which is required to be submitted in numerous copies. This effort takes a great deal of time. It also requires attention to be sure that the copying machine doesn't go haywire and give you crooked or bad quality copies.

### Disclosure Notice

The bid document should have a clause that allows you to restrict the usage of your proposal information to government evaluation purposes only. If the clause isn't a part of the bid document, write and ask the government contact for clarification. Refer to FAR 52.215-12.

It is a good idea to use this restriction since it may keep the public and your competition from getting their hands on your proposal. The FAR instructs you to mark the title page with the following statement:

> This proposal or quotation includes data that shall not be disclosed outside the Government and shall not be duplicated, used, or disclosed—in whole or in part—for any purpose other than to evaluate this proposal or quotation. If, however, a contract is awarded to this offeror or quoter as a result of—or in connection with—the submission of this data, the Government shall have the right to duplicate, use, or disclose the data to the extent provided in the resulting contract. This restriction does not limit the Governments's right to use information contained in this data if is obtained from another source without restriction. The data subject to this restriction are contained in sheets [insert numbers or other identification or sheets]."

You are also instructed to mark each sheet of data you want to restrict with the following statement:

> "Use or disclosure of data contained on this sheet is subject to the restriction on the title page of this proposal or quotation."

While this may seem to be a real chore, with today's word processing software it is as easy as entering a header or footer for each page.

### Tabs and Binders

Obviously you need something to package the finished product. If the government has not given you specific direction on binders, three-ring notebook style binders are quite handy. They are easy to work with and allow the review team to disassemble them. Which leads to another suggestion: that you identify your company name in the footer or header of each page. That way if the proposal is disassembled, it is still identifiable.

You will also need some type of tab or divider to identify sections. You can use tab indexes available at your local office supply store, or you can order printed ones (be sure to factor in lead time for printing). Whatever you choose, be sure to allow time for ordering or typing the titles so that they are ready in time for proposal assembly. You will also need labels for the proposal volumes.

### Assembly

By now you should have everything done and be ready to assemble the numerous copies of the required volumes. Find a quiet, unoccupied area or office. Again, attention to detail is very important. The proposal must be assembled in the correct order and include all pages. All copies of all volumes must be identical.

This may sound like a simple task. If it does, consider the fact that if you are required to submit 10 copies of four volumes, each containing 250 pages—not unlikely, by the way—you are going to be working with 10,000 sheets of paper. Laying out 40 notebooks requires a lot of space. It is also very easy to get confused or knock something off the table.

### Delivery

Be sure you know what is to be delivered, when it is to be delivered, where it is to be delivered, and how it is to be delivered. Then plan accordingly. This may involve your delivering the proposal personally. A lot of companies do just that, and with just cause since so much is at stake. Remember, if your proposal arrives late, it may be considered nonresponsive and all your efforts have been wasted.

## Maintaining the Team Spirit

Maintaining the team spirit is very important to the proposal process. Your best people are going to be working long hours, absorbing extra duties, and ignoring their families for a sustained period of time. In other words they are rendering services beyond the call of duty. It behooves you to make this experience as pleasant as possible.

If long hours keep them past supper time, spring for pizza or burgers. Monitor individuals for burnout. It is better to send them home for an evening's rest than to have them speed through a crucial section writing junk.

Completion of the proposal effort is a time for celebration. Give your team the afternoon off. Take them out to dinner. Successful award of a contract is also cause for celebration. Above all, strive to maintain a sense of unity and commitment if you want to be successful at proposal writing and subsequently become a successful government contractor.

# 8
# Setting Your Price

It's worth remembering that the purpose of this whole exercise is not only to make you into the best supplier the government ever had but also to bring you a profit! You should try to be the best supplier, of course, because competition for government contracts can be stiff, and being the best supplier is probably what it will take for you to win. But for you to be a good supplier, you have to stay in business. And that means you have to set the price for what you have to sell wisely, efficiently, and—always—profitably. Naming your price in government contracting is much like price setting in any other business, but with a few unique wrinkles.

## Make It or Buy It?

In order to establish a price for your goods or services you must first know how much the good or service costs. Obviously, the lower your cost, the lower your price can be. In the world of competitive procurement your cost and price must be the best if you expect to get the business. Therefore, you should carefully consider everything you do and everything that is required of you in the bid document as a potential candidate for a make or buy decision. Even if you have always fabricated the dispensing valve handle on your ice cream machine, ask yourself these four questions:

1. Can someone else manufacture the handle to meet the specifications?
2. Who is this supplier?

3. Can the supplier manufacture it less expensively than you?
4. Can the supplier meet your delivery requirements?

You may be surprised at the answers to these questions. There just may be a qualified source that doesn't have the same costs as you do. Of course, there are other considerations such as design priority, convenience, quality compliance, etc., but don't discount the possibility that your cost may not be the lowest.

Anything and everything can be purchased, from raw material and electronic components to engineering support and testing and training services. Once you have identified a list of viable candidates for make or buy consideration, the next step should be to assess your in-house capabilities. The following list of questions will help you with this assessment.

1. Do you have people available who are qualified to perform the task?
2. Do you have the necessary equipment to perform the task?
3. Do you have the time to perform the task?
4. Do you have the money to perform the task?
5. How will your competition perform the task?

If you answer yes to questions 1 through 4, then the task under consideration needs further evaluation as something you can "do" or "make" in house. If you feel reasonably certain that the competition views the task as a make decision, this further supports the need for in-house production. In other words, if they can make it in house, you definitely need to know whether you can and if not, why not. Perhaps production of the unit doesn't fit into your current schedule and you have no alternative but to buy it. The evaluation should basically tell you how much it will cost you to do or make it in house. Once you know this you have a rough idea of what it will cost your competition to make it.

You can now proceed to the final step in the decision-making process, which is to see what it will cost to buy the task. If you can make it cheaper and fulfill your contractual obligations, you make it. If you can buy it cheaper and fulfill your contractual obligations, you buy it.

If you answer no to *any* of the first four questions, then the candidate task needs further evaluation as something you may buy.

Your concern about the competition's intentions to make, do, or buy is simply that if they can make it, it is possible that you can also. If you feel reasonably certain that the competition views the task as a buy decision, that is not necessarily a consideration. Your job is to find the lowest cost, period.

When analyzing a candidate for buy, remember that you are dealing with a situation that you will be able to control less effectively than if it were a make. Since you are dealing with an unknown quantity when buying from someone else, as opposed to making it yourself, the process for evaluating a buy decision is somewhat different and more involved.

Once you have identified sources for purchased parts or services your assessment should include the following considerations:

- *What is the history of the company?* Have they been a manufacturer of this product or a supplier of this service for many years or are they the new kid on the block? Generally, you want a well-established company, although a latecomer with new and improved ideas may be better in some cases.
- *What is the company's financial position?* Are they on solid ground or are they in bankruptcy proceedings? Obviously, you want a company that will be around long enough to finish the job.
- *What is the size of the company?* Will your order be insignificant in their business plans, or will it be a major order for the company? The more important you are to the supplier, the more influence you will have when it comes time to negotiate.
- *Have you done business with this company before?* If you have, how are they to deal with? Are there always roadblocks you have to get around, or do they go out of their way to cooperate? This is a crucial concern, as even a company that passes all the other qualifications with flying colors may not be worth dealing with if they constantly try to fight you on everything.
- *Can their product or service meet the government specifications?* If you have doubts, it is best to clarify the situation now. Selling to the government isn't easy—if it were, you wouldn't be reading this. You don't need a supplier who, when it is time to meet the government's inspection, can't measure up.
- *What is the supplier's delivery history?* Are they always on time or always late? As noted previously, on-time delivery is very important in government contracting. You must be able to rely on your suppliers to do it at least as well as you.
- *Are they willing to make a commitment to your project?* If they are enthusiastic, that's great. If they act uninterested, there must be a reason. You don't have to be a mind reader to know when you aren't welcome; assessing how much willingness somebody has to put forth

the needed effort is a little tougher, but may pay off down the road when the going gets tough.

- *Are they willing to accept your terms and conditions as is or with minor adjustments?* If you can't iron out the terms and conditions up front, do you want to do business with them?

This may seem like an awful lot of investigation to go through, but the best source is the most qualified source. The most qualified source is the supplier who will deliver on-time, quality products that meet the specifications and who is a pleasure to do business with. The last thing you need in a government contract on a tight schedule is someone who delivers late, provides faulty merchandise, or is always a pain in your side to do business with. You will have enough to worry about without these added headaches.

## Who Decides Whether to Make or Buy?

The decision whether to make or buy requires input from various personnel within the entire organization, beginning with the engineering and manufacturing personnel who probably have the best idea of what your manufacturing capabilities are. The production control and scheduling departments can assess run times and shop loading requirements. Finally, the purchasing, accounting, and human resources departments can give you an estimate of the cost and availability of materials and personnel. The team concept developed in the review and proposal stages carries over very well into the make or buy process. Of course, someone has to have the final say. This person is usually the chief executive of the company. But it is a wise CEO who actively seeks input from personnel responsible for the daily functions of the company and objectively listens and evaluates that input.

## Negotiating with Vendors

Negotiation with your vendors or suppliers to obtain the lowest possible cost is an enormous task most often left in the capable hands of a purchasing agent or purchasing manager. Also, the time constraints imposed by the government for submitting the bid seldom allow for detailed meetings and haggling with your vendors. Therefore, you should identify the big-ticket items and ensure that a concentrated effort is made to negotiate their cost. An engine costs considerably more than a door latch and is proportionately a bigger part of the total cost. A price that is "fair" for a door latch can be lived with. A price that is "fair" for an engine requires negotiation.

Negotiations for items or services of considerable value can take on the characteristics of a three-act play. First there is the introduction, where the principal characters are introduced to each other. This usually begins with a telephone conversation wherein the vendor introduces himself as someone who has something you need (a product or service), or you introduce yourself to the vendor as someone who has something they need (your business).

At this stage, you carefully feel each other out. Perhaps you are invited to visit and see how things operate, or you extend your own invitation. This leads to some wining and dining and the next thing you know everybody is the best of friends.

Then comes act two, the conflict. Your vendor states that he can supply you the good or service for a set price. You say you cannot possibly be competitive with that cost and the vendor will have to do better (is this starting to sound familiar?). You bicker back and forth, each gives and takes a little, and you decide that maybe you need to think a little longer about the situation.

Act three is the denouement. Whoever you decide upon, you now have to heal the wounds brought on by negotiations for cost, terms, and conditions. Each makes a commitment to the other to perform successfully, and a team is formed for the good of all.

## To Ensure a Happy Ending

While the above scenario may be a little bit of an exaggeration, it often seems to be the way negotiations go. The following suggestions are offered for improved negotiating:

- Remember that both sides need to come out a winner. This will require give and take by both parties.
- Instill in your vendor a confidence that you can do the job better than anyone else and require the same of them.
- Let vendors know who their competition is. It may get you a better cost.
- Be up-front with your vendor about any doubt you have in their capabilities or any deficiencies in their product or service.

- Be honest and sincere about yourself and your business. No one likes to do business with someone about whom they have doubts.

A final word about vendor negotiations: There are times when the government will specify exactly who the source will be for a product or service (this is known as a sole source). This naturally shoots the negotiation process right in the foot. When this happens, remember that the bid document should specify exactly what it is you have to purchase. The price of that product or service should not differ between you and your competition.

## The Parts of the Sum

Figuring out what something costs so that you can establish a price for it may be the most inexact part of the bid process. A good friend who is a CPA and former CEO for a defense contractor had this to say about costing: "There is nothing exact about costing. It will take *all* of your judgment skills."

Another way to view costing is as the "Science of the Unknowns." There are general guidelines to make sure you cost everything. The government requires you to provide cost or pricing certification so that they can analyze your costing. But there are no guidelines to tell you how to cost everything.

As in most of the tasks we have discussed in previous chapters, the first step is to gather as much information as possible. The more you know about what it is the government wants and how you can provide it, the more accurate your cost will be. Take the information you have gathered and structure a bill of material for the product or service. This allows everyone to work from the same document. It also forces you to organize the costing effort. Provided below are some basic tips for costing.

### Material

Your bill of material identifies components you plan to fabricate and components you plan to purchase. For fabricated parts you will need to make an estimate of how much raw material is required.

Be sure to include a scrap factor for raw material. You will undoubtedly have some normal scrap from the fabrication operations and will at some point in time have some scrap from production errors.

You may already have some raw material in stock leftover from another project. This material may have been bought at a cheaper rate than is currently available. At what quantity will you get a price break? Do you buy the 900 pounds of steel you need at 35 cents per pound or go ahead and buy 1000 pounds at 30 cents per pound?

Purchased components generally follow the same rules. You may already have some parts in stock at a cheaper price. Price breaks will need to be evaluated. If you need 25 spatulas you may be able to buy 100 cheaper, or there may be a minimum order quantity of 50.

You will also want to inquire about a restocking charge. Since your estimate is not 100 percent accurate you may overbuy and want to return the excess goods. The restock charge may help you decide which vendor you use.

## Labor

The labor involved in your effort is only an estimate. You may think it will take 50 hours of manufacturing time to make the product, or 20 hours to prepare the report. In reality it may take 55 hours or 25 hours. A five-hour overrun in preparing the report will not seriously impact your profit. A five-hour overrun on a per unit basis for 1000 units will make a substantial dent in your profit.

Whatever the task, hourly wages will have to be computed for each skill involved. You should consider time for a learning curve if the good or service is something you are unfamiliar with. The first 100 units may take an extra two hours per unit. After that time, labor may even taper off to below your expectations. You should be so lucky.

What about the cost of training to acquire new skills? What is the duration of the job? Will there be wage and benefit increases during that time? What is the cost of benefits, taxes, worker's compensation?

You are most likely accustomed to at least some of these costing techniques from the normal operation of your business. But in government contracting your customer's demands—and ability to enforce those demands—are steep. You have little room for serious error.

## Overhead

Overhead can vary considerably from one company to the other. A detailed discussion of overhead would not be of benefit to all the readers of this book. The following suggestions provide general guidance.

- Know your accounting system and know what it is that you cost as overhead. The government will want to review this information at some point in time and the more confident you are in communicating what your overhead costs are the better your chances are that the auditor will agree with you.

- Know what it is that the government will not allow as overhead. Study the FARs. Despite what you may have read in the paper or heard, memberships to country clubs will not be allowed as overhead on a government contract.

## Special Cost Considerations

The following areas are of special concern when costing a job. Although they are a part of the three cost categories discussed above, they should be considered separately because they can have a significant impact on cost.

### Data

The government is obsessed with the need to create reports, analyses, and other forms of documentation about a particular good or service. These range from relatively simple monthly summaries of your progress to reliability-centered maintenance analyses that may be separate projects in themselves. Sometimes the cost of the data is insignificant to the total cost of the project. Other times it may be a big part of the cost.

Above all, do not discount the data's importance in the successful performance of your contract. In government contracting, it is not enough to merely do a good job. You have to have the documentation to back you up. Most contracts provide clauses for not accepting the product if the data is unacceptable or late in delivery.

When costing the data keep in mind that the cost extends beyond the actual preparation time. There will be time required to review and verify the data with the government. This can take the form of a desktop review, which doesn't cost you anything if performed by the government at their facilities, to a formal review and verification at your facilities, which may take weeks or perhaps months. You have to plan for the reviews, participate in them, and conduct follow-up actions. All of this review process costs, and often the length of time involved is an unknown.

### Testing

If your project requires testing, consider the following. First, testing can be a make or buy decision. If you are not qualified or experienced in testing, it is best left to those who specialize in it. If you do plan to perform the testing yourself be sure to cost labor, consumables, facilities and equipment, and transportation of the product and test equipment.

If the testing will be performed at a government facility, what schedule will they allow? Can you test 24 hours a day seven days a week, or from 8 a.m. to 5 p.m. Monday through Friday? You may have to cost for food and lodging of your test personnel, depending on the provisions of the contract. Also keep in mind that if you have a test failure attributable to your design, you may be required to retest at your expense if you cannot work the problem out with the government.

### Consumables

Consumables are the everyday supplies used in creating your product or service. This could be toner for the copying machine or solder for welding. Consumables may be a part of your overhead costs. Look at the specifics of the project to see whether they may create an increase in that cost. Are you going to be doing a considerable amount of welding, which requires welding rod and gasses? Are you manufacturing something that has to be preserved before shipment? Are there special cleaning processes that require more or different chemicals?

### Capital Expenditures

Costing new equipment into a project can effectively put you out of the competition. In general, you should already have the major pieces of equipment you need to complete the contract. If new equipment is required, can it be used for other jobs after this one? If so, do you already have the work, or are you confident you can get the work?

You may want to absorb part of the cost of the equipment in this project and spread it across other projects. You may want to consider selling the equipment after the project is over. If so, how much do you cost to the project? These are all difficult questions.

## Cost Evaluation and Analysis

You are not the only one that is concerned with the exact nature of your costs and how you arrived at them. the government, too, is very interested. The FARs contain guidelines for the contracting officer to use in determining whether a cost is allowable and how to perform a cost analysis. If you are going to pass that contracting officer's inspection, you need to know those requirements, at least in outline.

### Is the Cost Allowable?

Basically if the cost is incurred within the terms of the contract, is reasonable, and can be allocated to the contract, it is an allowable cost. A cost is *reasonable* if its nature and amount does not exceed that which would be incurred by a prudent person in the conduct of competitive business. That is a subjective definition of reasonable, of course, but if you try to follow it in the same spirit in which you operate your business, you should not go wrong.

The method of determining whether a cost can be *allocated* to a contract is somewhat more objective. A cost is allocable to a contract if it meets these three criteria:

1. It is incurred specifically for the contract.
2. It benefits both the contract and other work, and can be distributed to them in a reasonable proportion.
3. It is necessary to the overall operation of the business, although a direct relationship to any particular cost objective cannot be shown.

### How Is the Cost Analyzed?

FAR 48 CFR 15.805-3 provides the contracting officer with guidelines for cost analysis. Briefly, these guidelines allow for cost analysis using any of the following methods:

- Verification of cost or pricing data and evaluation of cost elements. This includes the necessity for and reasonableness of the costs, projection of the offeror's cost trends on the basis of current and historical data, a technical appraisal of the cost element (labor, material, facilities, etc.), and the application of indirect cost and labor rates.
- Evaluation of the effect of the offeror's current practices on future costs.
- Comparison of the offeror's proposed costs with previous costs, other estimates, forecasts, etc.

- Verification that the offeror's costs are in accordance with prescribed cost principles and standards.
- Review to see if any costs have not been submitted.

## Setting Your Price

All right. You have established your cost of the good or service being purchased, and you are now down to the final element—that is, profit. This element of cost is purely judgmental. But you will have to ask yourself the following four questions:

1. How much profit do you need?
2. How much profit will still allow you to be the low bidder?
3. How do you feel about your cost effort?
4. How much risk are you willing to take?

My CPA friend poses the question this way: "Do you want the job at this price? If it's just one dollar less; then you don't want the job. That's how much profit you add to cost."

It would be nice if you could just add a set percentage to your cost as profit and not worry about it. But it's not that easy. There are a number of things you should consider, including:

- Can you expect to incur price increases from your suppliers? If you have foreign suppliers, you must factor in the exchange rate of the dollar. The price of raw material may fluctuate with the economy.
- How are you going to buy materials? In what quantities? You may not know this yet since you don't know if the government will exceed their minimum order quantity. Being the successful bidder may give you leverage to get an even lower price from a vendor.
- What influence does the competition have on your price? What do you think they might bid? If they have a history of bidding on this product, you might be able to get an idea of whether they typically bid high or low.
- What is the present and future economic state of the country? Is inflation running rampant or relatively stable?
- And finally, how complex is the item you are bidding? If it is a soft-serve ice cream machine, you can probably get a fairly accurate cost for it. If it is a Stealth Fighter, your degree of accuracy will probably be less.

## Required Cost Certification or Pricing Data

In addition to satisfying your own internal requirements for cost documentation, there are several government forms you will have to fill out to convey that information to the buying agency.

The FAR, 48 CFR 15-804, requires that the contracting officer get cost certification or pricing data from the bidder before awarding any negotiated contract expected to exceed $100,000. The contracting officer also has the option of asking for this information for award amounts over $25,000.

This Certificate of Current Cost or Pricing Data basically states that you certify to the best of your knowledge the cost or pricing data submitted in support of your bid is accurate, complete, and current as of the date that price negotiations are concluded. The form for submitting cost or pricing data is SF 1411, Contract Pricing Proposal Cover Sheet (see Figure 8-1). On this form you will have to detail your cost for each line item listed in Section B of the bid document. The cost of each line item is broken down by cost element (materials, labor, etc.). You must also provide supporting documentation for each cost element such as vendor quotations, labor estimates, and your method of calculation. Therefore, it is necessary to keep good records of your costing effort.

Certain conditions may allow you an exemption from or waiver of submission of certified cost or pricing data. An exemption or waiver is allowed when:

- The pricing is based on adequate price competition. Price competition exists if, when offers are solicited, two or more responsible offerors can satisfy the government's requirements and respond to the offer, and the offerors compete independently of each other. Price competition is adequate unless it denies a qualified candidate the opportunity to bid, the lowest price is unreasonable, or the low offeror has such an advantage as to prohibit competition.
- The price is based on established catalog or market prices of commercial items sold in substantial quantities to the general public. Established catalog prices must be documented in a form regularly maintained by the manufacturer, such as a price sheet or catalog. An item is sold in substantial quantities when the quantities are sufficient to establish a genuine commercial market.
- The price is set by law or regulation. If the cost of the item is regularly reviewed or ruled upon by a government body, then it is said to be set by law or regulation.

**CONTRACT PRICING PROPOSAL COVER SHEET**

1. SOLICITATION/CONTRACT/MODIFICATION NO.

FORM APPROVED OMB NO. 3090-0116

NOTE: This form is used in contract actions if submission of cost or pricing data is required. *(See FAR 15.804-6(b))*

2. NAME AND ADDRESS OF OFFEROR *(Include ZIP Code)*

3A. NAME AND TITLE OF OFFEROR'S POINT OF CONTACT

3B. TELEPHONE NO.

4. TYPE OF CONTRACT ACTION *(Check)*

| | |
|---|---|
| A. NEW CONTRACT | D. LETTER CONTRACT |
| B. CHANGE ORDER | E. UNPRICED ORDER |
| C. PRICE REVISION/ REDETERMINATION | F. OTHER *(Specify)* |

5. TYPE OF CONTRACT *(Check)*

☐ FFP ☐ CPFF ☐ CPIF ☐ CPAF
☐ FPI ☐ OTHER *(Specify)*

6. PROPOSED COST *(A+B=C)*

| A. COST | B. PROFIT/FEE | C. TOTAL |
|---|---|---|
| $ | $ | $ |

7. PLACE(S) AND PERIOD(S) OF PERFORMANCE

8. List and reference the identification, quantity and total price proposed for each contract line item. A line item cost breakdown supporting this recap is required unless otherwise specified by the Contracting Officer. *(Continue on reverse, and then on plain paper, if necessary. Use same headings.)*

| A. LINE ITEM NO. | B. IDENTIFICATION | C. QUANTITY | D. TOTAL PRICE | E. REF. |
|---|---|---|---|---|
| | | | | |

9. PROVIDE NAME, ADDRESS, AND TELEPHONE NUMBER FOR THE FOLLOWING *(If available)*

A. CONTRACT ADMINISTRATION OFFICE

B. AUDIT OFFICE

10. WILL YOU REQUIRE THE USE OF ANY GOVERNMENT PROPERTY IN THE PERFORMANCE OF THIS WORK? *(If "Yes," identify)*

☐ YES ☐ NO

11A. DO YOU REQUIRE GOVERNMENT CONTRACT FINANCING TO PERFORM THIS PROPOSED CONTRACT? *(If "Yes," complete Item 11B)*

☐ YES ☐ NO

11B. TYPE OF FINANCING *(√ one)*

☐ ADVANCE PAYMENTS ☐ PROGRESS PAYMENTS
☐ GUARANTEED LOANS

12. HAVE YOU BEEN AWARDED ANY CONTRACTS OR SUBCONTRACTS FOR THE SAME OR SIMILAR ITEMS WITHIN THE PAST 3 YEARS? *(If "Yes," identify item(s), customer(s) and contract number(s))*

☐ YES ☐ NO

13. IS THIS PROPOSAL CONSISTENT WITH YOUR ESTABLISHED ESTIMATING AND ACCOUNTING PRACTICES AND PROCEDURES AND FAR PART 31 COST PRINCIPLES? *(If "No," explain)*

☐ YES ☐ NO

14. COST ACCOUNTING STANDARDS BOARD (CASB) DATA *(Public Law 91-379 as amended and FAR PART 30)*

A. WILL THIS CONTRACT ACTION BE SUBJECT TO CASB REGULATIONS? *(If "No," explain in proposal)*

☐ YES ☐ NO

B. HAVE YOU SUBMITTED A CASB DISCLOSURE STATEMENT *(CASB DS-1 or 2)? (If "Yes," specify in proposal the office to which submitted and if determined to be adequate)*

☐ YES ☐ NO

C. HAVE YOU BEEN NOTIFIED THAT YOU ARE OR MAY BE IN NONCOMPLIANCE WITH YOUR DISCLOSURE STATEMENT OR COST ACCOUNTING STANDARDS? *(If "Yes," explain in proposal)*

☐ YES ☐ NO

D. IS ANY ASPECT OF THIS PROPOSAL INCONSISTENT WITH YOUR DISCLOSED PRACTICES OR APPLICABLE COST ACCOUNTING STANDARDS? *(If "Yes," explain in proposal)*

☐ YES ☐ NO

This proposal is submitted in response to the RFP contract, modification, etc. in Item 1 and reflects our best estimates and/or actual costs as of this date.

15. NAME AND TITLE *(Type)*

16. NAME OF FIRM

17. SIGNATURE

18. DATE OF SUBMISSION

NSN 7540-01-142-9845 1411 101 **STANDARD FORM 1411** (10-83)
Prescribed by GSA
FAR (48 CFR) 53.215-2(c)

U.S. GOVERNMENT PRINTING OFFICE : 1984 O - 437-443

**Figure 8-1.** Contract Pricing Proposal Cover Sheet (SF 1411) for certifying pricing data.

The FAR details each of these exemptions. If you feel that you may qualify for an exemption or waiver, research the FAR. The form for requesting an exemption is SF 1412, Claim for Exemption from Submission of Certified Cost or Pricing Data (see Figure 8-2). On or with the SF 1412 you will have to provide a copy of your catalog or pricing sheet; the sales period covered for the pricing information provided; the amount of sales to the government or for government use, sales to the general public at the catalog price, and all sales to the general public that were discounted from the catalog price. You will also have to identify the lowest price you sold the item for during the sales period identified.

**CLAIM FOR EXEMPTION FROM SUBMISSION OF CERTIFIED COST OR PRICING DATA**

FORM APPROVED OMB NO. **3090-0116**

| 1. OFFEROR *(Name, address, ZIP Code)* | 3. SOLICITATION NO. | |
|---|---|---|
| | 4. ITEM OF SUPPLIES AND/OR SERVICES TO BE FURNISHED | |
| 2. DIVISION(S) AND LOCATION(S) WHERE WORK IS TO BE PERFORMED | 5. QUANTITY | 6. TOTAL AMOUNT PROPOSED FOR ITEM $ |

By submission of this form the offeror claims exemption from requirements for submitting certified cost or pricing data on the basis that the price offered is based on an established catalog or market price of a commercial item sold in substantial quantities to the general public or is a price set by law or regulation (see FAR 15.804-3). Complete Section I, II, or III below as applicable.

**SECTION I – CATALOG PRICE** *(See Instructions for items 7 thru 11 on reverse.)*

| 7. CATALOG IDENTIFICATION AND DATE | 8. SALES PERIOD COVERED FROM | TO |
|---|---|---|

| 9. CATEGORIES OF SALES | TOTAL UNITS SOLD* | 10. REMARKS |
|---|---|---|
| a. U.S. Government sales | | |
| b. Sales at catalog price to general public | | |
| c. Other sales to general public | | |

**If your accounting system does not provide precise information, insert your best estimate and explain the basis for it in Item 10, REMARKS. Continue on a separate sheet, if necessary.*

11. LIST THREE SALES OF THE ITEM OFFERED

| SALES CATEGORY | DATE | NO. OF UNITS SOLD | PRICE/UNIT |
|---|---|---|---|
| a. ☐ B ☐ C | | | $ |
| b. ☐ B ☐ C | | | $ |
| c. ☐ B ☐ C | | | $ |

**SECTION II – MARKET PRICE** *(See Instructions for item 12 on reverse.)*

12. SET FORTH THE SOURCE AND DATE OR PERIOD OF THE MARKET QUOTATION OR OTHER BASE FOR MARKET PRICE, THE BASE AMOUNT, AND APPLICABLE DISCOUNTS.

**SECTION III – LAW OR REGULATION** *(See Instructions for item 13 on reverse.)*

13. IDENTIFY THE LAW OR REGULATION ESTABLISHING THE PRICE OFFERED

REPRESENTATION *(See Instructions for item 14 on reverse.)*

The offeror represents that all statements made above and on attachments submitted are accurate and are submitted for the purpose of claiming exemption from requirements for submitting certified cost or pricing data. The offeror also represents that, except as stated in an attachment, a like claim for exemption involving the same or a substantially similar item has not been denied by a Government Contracting Officer within the last 2 years. Pending consideration of the proposal supported by this submission and, if this proposal or a modification of it is accepted by the Government, until the expiration of 3 years from the date of final payment under a contract resulting from this proposal, the Contracting Officer or any other authorized employee of the United States Government is granted access to books, records, documents, and other supporting data that will permit verification of the claim.

| 14. TYPED NAME, TITLE, AND FIRM | 15. SIGNATURE | 16. DATE OF SUBMISSION |
|---|---|---|
| | | |

NSN 7540-01-142-9846
1412-101

**STANDARD FORM 1412** (10-83)
Prescribed by GSA
FAR (48 CFR) 53.215-2(b)

**Figure 8-2.** Claim for Exemption from Cost or Pricing Data (SF 1412).

# 9
# Signed, Sealed, and Delivered

## What to Check Before You Mail

The final leg in our journey to be responsive has begun. All the hours or research, preliminary design, costing, and writing, are now recorded in a comprehensive document that details to the government how, what, when, and where you will provide for the government's needs, and for how much. At this point you should ask yourself two questions:

First, have I provided a response that meets the requirements detailed in Sections L and M?

Second, have I established a price that is competitive and profitable to me?

If you need help in answering either of these questions, go back and review Chapters 7 and 8. Otherwise, it is time to wrap up the package and deliver it to the government.

The checklist in Figure 9-1 can be used to help you ensure that your package is ready to mail or deliver. The ten questions are discussed below.

1. *Have representations and certifications been completed properly?* Review Section K to be sure that addresses and names have been filled in, yes and no blocks have been checked correctly, and all information has been entered as required.

2. *Have all amendments been acknowledged?* Block 11 of Standard Form 30 gives instructions for acknowledging amendments. Basically, there are three methods of acknowledgement.

**Final Checklist**

1. Have representations and certifications been completed properly?
2. Have all amendments been acknowledged?
3. Has the offer been signed by an authorized official of your firm?
4. Have the correct number of copies been made?
5. Have all pages of each copy been accounted for?
6. Have copies been separated into volumes in accordance with government instructions?
7. Are the volumes labeled properly?
8. Has the offer been properly packaged for delivery?
9. Has the package been labeled in accordance with government instructions?
10. Have delivery arrangements been made?

**Figure 9-1.** Ten items to check before mailing or delivering your proposal.

You can complete Items 8 and 15 of SF 30 and return a specified number of copies. Or, you can identify the amendment number and date in the space provided on the offer and return it with each copy of the offer submitted. Or, you can return a separate letter or telegram that includes a reference to the solicitation and amendment numbers.

It is important to note that if your acknowledgement is not received at the place designated for the receipt of offers prior to the hour and date specified, it may result in rejection of your offer.

3. *Has the offer been signed by an authorized official of your firm?* Be sure the person signing the offer in the space provided is authorized to legally bind your company to a contract.

4. *Have the correct number of copies been made?* Read the submission instructions in Section L carefully. Often there are separate paragraphs detailing how many copies of each volume are needed.

Don't stop at the first paragraph of instruction. The administrative contracting officer may need one copy of the pricing volume and one copy of the technical volume, and the review team may need three copies of the technical volume and no copies of the pricing volume.

5. *Have all pages of each copy been accounted for?* Be sure that all pages of each copy are present and accounted for. There is nothing like

reading a mystery novel and finding out the last page is missing. We don't want to frustrate the reviewer.

We also don't want to answer a review question that asks, "What are you talking about?" or "Where did you discuss this?" It is embarrassing to write back that we inadvertently left that section out of the copy. It also reflects poorly on our business practices.

6. *Have copies been separated into volumes in accordance with government instructions?* Remember the proposal structure requirements detailed in Figure 7-1. It is important that each volume contains specifically what the government expects to see in that volume. If they have to go looking for it in another volume, you may be considered nonresponsive.

7. *Are the volumes labeled properly?* Follow any directions on labeling exactly as given. This is not the time for improvisation. If you are instructed to list the solicitation number, volume number, and volume name, do it in that order.

8. *Has the offer been properly packaged for delivery?* If you are going to mail or ship your offer, be sure to protect it from damage due to shipment or the environment. An offer that arrives in pieces, or is wet and unreadable, is your fault. It is also nonresponsive. Again, follow any government directions. They may tell you to use bubblewrap and a shoestring. Do it.

9. *Has the package been labeled in accordance with the government instructions?* The government may include labeling instructions for both the inside and outside of the package. An example of a labeling instruction for inside the package is as follows:

> The inside wrapping shall bear the notation: To be opened only by (insert the name of the cognizant auditor). Do not open before (insert time and date established for receipt of offers). Notice: This is a source selection procurement.

Directions for labeling the outside of the package may include identifying the solicitation number and date and time established for receipt of offers. Often, the government provides a label for this information.

10. *Have delivery arrangements been made?* You need to plan for delivery whether you are going to deliver the offer in person or mail or ship it. Be sure to allow plenty of time for your offer to arrive by the specified date and time.

If you are delivering it in person, remember that finding your way around a government facility or military base may take some time. You might want to deliver the offer the day before the submission date, and then return at the time of opening, if you wish to be there when the bids are read.

If you are mailing or using a shipping service, be sure you have the right amount of postage and have allowed some extra time for delays. If the bid is not there when it is supposed to be, you can be declared nonresponsive.

In accordance with the FAR, if you mail your offer by registered or certified mail it should be mailed no later than five calendar days before the receipt date specified. If you mail your offer using postal service express mail next day service, it should be mailed not later than 5 p.m. at the place of mailing two working days prior to the date specified for receipt.

## The Government's Evaluation Process

The evaluation process is where the government begins its review of your offer.

For an IFB using the sealed bidding process, evaluation is relatively simple. The bids are opened at the designated time and reviewed for completeness. At this time the low bidder will be announced and will most likely end up being awarded the contract. However, all bids are examined for mistakes by the contracting officer. If there is an apparent mistake, or if the contracting officer has reason to believe that a mistake has been made, there are provisions in the FAR for correction. Only after all bids have been examined will a contract be awarded.

If the solicitation does not use the sealed bidding process, but seeks response through the form of a proposal and discussion, it is said to be a negotiated contract. Negotiation is defined in the FAR as

> a procedure that includes the receipt of proposals from offerors, permits bargaining, and usually affords an opportunity for offerors to revise their offers before award of a contract. Bargaining in the sense of discussion, persuasion, alteration of initial assumptions and positions, and give-and-take may apply to price, schedule, technical requirements, type of contract, or other terms of a proposed contract.

Proposal evaluation begins the negotiation stage of a contract. The purpose of the evaluation is to assess the proposal and the offeror's ability to successfully perform the requirements of the contract.

Section M of the bid document has detailed the evaluation criteria to be used. If we have developed our outline and proposal text in accordance with Section L, we should have covered all the areas of evaluation detailed in Section M, to the degree necessary to make our proposal responsive. And if we have costed our product or service to the best of our ability, we should also be considered competitive, which opens the door for written and oral discussion of our offer with the government.

## The Question and Answer Stage

Most bid documents contain a clause stating that contract award may be made without conducting further discussion with any offeror. However, the government usually cannot resist the temptation of trying to drive the cost down as far as they can. Thus, if you have been responsive, and are competitive, expect to participate in a round of written and/or oral discussions concerning your proposal.

### Oral Discussion

In the case of oral discussion, you will be notified that the government intends to conduct a meeting with you to clarify questions they have regarding your proposal. Usually the meeting will be at the facilities of the agency buying your product or service. This is likely for two reasons: First, the travel expense to meet with them is yours. Second, they are probably conducting these discussions with more than one offeror, so there is a concern on their part for expediency as well as expense.

In any case, you should receive a list of questions that they intend to discuss. You should also be given a fair amount of time to prepare the answers.

The government will ask for confirmation that you are coming and will ask for a list of who will be attending the meeting. Take only those personnel necessary to intelligently discuss the questions and answers. You want to convey to the government your understanding of the requirements and clear up any concerns they have. This is not the time for a parade.

### Written Discussion

In the case of written discussion, you will receive a letter notifying you of the government's concerns. The letter will provide a listing of their questions as well as a date for response. Again, you should be allowed a fair amount of time to respond.

Keep in mind that the questions are being asked because someone either does not understand something or cannot find what they are looking for. There could be a misunderstanding about how the information you have given them meets the requirements of the bid document or because a response to an evaluation factor cannot be found. Or, perhaps you have provided too much or too little information in response to an evaluation factor.

Communication is a key consideration during this stage. No matter how stupid you think the question is, you still have to answer it. Be tactful. Just because you think the information being sought in the question was contained in the original text of the proposal doesn't mean it was really there.

It could be that the page was missing or misplaced in the copy. Or possibly, the reviewer read the material and didn't understand it, or the reviewer read someone else's material and thought it was yours, or any number of things.

Approach each question objectively and with an open mind to communicating the answer in the best manner possible.

## Understanding the Question

Be sure to read each question carefully. The questions may provide you with insight into what the reviewer is looking for in response to the evaluation factor.

If you don't understand the question, get further clarification. Usually this can be done by phoning the contracting officer and explaining that you would like to discuss the question with the reviewer. Try this first and if the contracting officer gives you instructions to address your questions in writing or to follow up in writing, be sure to do so.

If you find that you are being asked a question that you are certain you addressed with a detailed and complete answer, don't panic. Often the reviewer will ask the same question of every offeror. This is a way of confirming what is being proposed by all parties. If an offeror is way off base in the proposal, and later claims the government did not treat the offeror fairly, the government can respond by showing that the question was asked of everybody for clarification.

You may also be asked a question because the reviewer simply could not find the answer. In this case referring the questioner to the section, and providing them with a copy of the text is the best way to answer.

You may need to rewrite parts of a section or even an entire section. This is permissible. I once had to rewrite a section twice. Now that I reflect on the situation, I realize that the failure to communicate adequately the first time was attributable to the fact that I was so well versed on the subject that my response was too generic. I assumed that whoever was reviewing the proposal understood it as well as I did. I left several details out figuring that they were automatically understood.

When I received the question the first time, I added more information but not enough to suit the reviewer. The question was asked again in more detail. This time I answered explicitly providing the step-by-step process for each phase, along with methodology for accomplishing the work, and who was responsible for each step, by position. Obviously this is what the reviewer wanted, because the question was not asked again and the company I was working for was ultimately awarded the contract.

## Answering the Question

Format is an important part of answering the questions. Be sure your answers are consistent, easy to read, and traceable to the original proposal text. The best method is to repeat the question word for word, and provide the answer below the question. Answer the question directly and take care not to commit for more than is required in the bid document. Sometimes you may feel that you did not provide enough information and want to add additional effort on your part to compensate, or perhaps to get an advantage on your competition. Remember that these answers become a part of your proposal text and you will be bound to provide the goods and services that you propose.

**Changing Your Answer.** You are allowed to change the wording of any text or rewrite any section to clarify your answer or include more information. When performing any modification to the original text, provide replacement pages along with instructions for the reviewer. An example of such an instruction would be as follows:

> Section 3.1 has been revised to answer Question 1. Remove pages 3-1 and 3-2 and replace with pages 3-1a and 3-2a enclosed.

**Getting Help.** You may have to enlist the aid of your suppliers to answer questions of a technical nature. Don't be afraid to ask them for help. They are the experts in what they supply and should be able to provide any text, calculations, or supporting documentation to answer the government's concerns.

If you need to provide calculations to support an answer, be sure to define the mathematical terms and equation(s) prior to presenting the numerical calculations.

If you need to supply supporting documentation such as vendor catalog sheets or test results, be sure to label them so that the reviewer clearly understands which question they address.

**Illustrations.** Another helpful way to answer questions is to include an illustration, chart, or table. Here we are following the old adage that says a picture is worth a thousand words. If you choose this approach, be sure to supplement the figure with some descriptive text that walks the reviewer through your reasoning.

**Cover Letters.** Finally, you need to preface your answers with a good cover letter. In the cover letter you should let the reader know you have received the questions, carefully reviewed the questions, and answered in what you feel is a clear and concise manner. You should also indicate the willingness to cooperate if the government has further questions or concerns. Figure 9-2 is a sample cover letter.

## BAFOs, LAFOs, and UFOs

When all questions from all offerors have been answered, and all written or oral discussion have been completed, the next step in the procurement process is for the contracting officer to issue a request for a *final offer* to all offerors who are still within the competitive range. The Best and Final Offer (BAFO) is the most common type of request. However, don't be surprised to see more than one request. That is, you may progress from a BAFO to a second BAFO and then to a Last and Final Offer (LAFO) or to anything else the government may want to preface "final offer" with. These I call UFOs, Unidentified Final Offers.

### Understanding the Final Offer

What does all this final offer process mean? It usually means that the field of competition has been narrowed by reviewing the original proposal text and the questions and answers. It usually means that you are technically responsive to the government requirements of the bid document. Essentially, you have reached the next rung on the ladder of being a successful government supplier.

XYZ Corporation
135 Crown Street
Somewhere, US 64023

July 14, 1993

Department of the Air Force
Your Favorite Air Base
Anywhere, US 39104

Attn: Contracting Officer

Dear Sir:

Subj: Response to Questions regarding Solicitation 123
Ref: Letter from (insert name, title), dated (insert date)

The XYZ Corporation is in receipt of the above-referenced letter.

Our staff has reviewed the questions contained therein, and we provide our response in the attachment to this letter. Note that each question in your letter is repeated, followed by our answer.

XYZ believes we have communicated our response to your questions in a clear and concise manner. However, should questions still exist upon your review of our response, we will happy to respond to them.

Sincerely,

Jane Doe
President

Enclosure

**Figure 9-2.** Sample covering letter to accompany answers to the government's questions during the discussion stage of proposal negotiations.

A review of the FAR (48 CFR 15.611) tells us that a final offer is to include the following:

- Notice that discussions with offerors are concluded
- Notice that this is an opportunity to submit your best and final offer
- A common cutoff date and time that provides a fair opportunity for submission of a written final offer
- Notice that if any modification is submitted, it is subject to the provisions for late submission, modifications, and withdrawals of proposals in the solicitation and it must be received by the date and time specified

The next paragraph of the FAR states that after receipt of BAFOs, the government should not reopen discussions with the offerors unless it is in the government's best interest to do so. This does often happen as the government receives more information that clarifies its requirements while you are in the process of preparing the BAFO. If discussions are reopened, which seems to be the trend these days, the contracting officer issues an additional request for final offer (UFO).

### Responding to the Final Offer

Now that we understand the purpose of a final offer, let's examine how we should respond. The first thing to do is to examine your questions and answers to see what impact, if any, they have on your cost and pricing. If you need to make changes to your bid, go ahead and do so. If there is no impact on your bid, the next step is to review your original cost and pricing.

Go back to your suppliers and let them know you have been requested to make a final offer. This is a good indication to them that you are a strong contender for the job. In turn they should reevaluate their cost and pricing and let you know of any changes.

It's important not to skip this step. Often, suppliers that are familiar with government contracting are very much aware of this final offer process. They may hold back some of the cost savings to be able to reduce their price to you when the time comes.

On the other hand, some suppliers give the best price going into the bid. Don't be disappointed if the suppliers' final offer is the same as the original. It never hurts to ask, and it never hurts to use the leverage that you have been requested to submit a final offer as a means of reducing your price to the government.

Once you have arrived at your best and final offer, the pricing in Section B of the bid document will have to be revised to indicate what your offer is. Be sure that you dot all the *i*'s and cross all the *t*'s just as you did in your original bid.

A final word of advice about final offers. In a negotiated competitive procurement, you may already be the low offeror. There is really no way to tell at this stage. Therefore, as we discussed in Chapter 8, ask yourself, "If I bid this job for one dollar less would I want it?" You are in business to make a profit. Don't sacrifice your goal just to say you are a government supplier.

## One Last Hurdle

By the time final offers have been received, the field of competition should be narrowed down to just a few offerors. At that time, the contracting officer will usually request a preaward survey of the offerors still under consideration.

A preaward survey is conducted by a team of government representatives. This team will come to your facilities and review your operations and equipment to determine your capabilities to perform if awarded a contract. Alternate survey methods include written correspondence or telephone conversations. The survey team will visit with your personnel who will be involved in the performance of the contract, review various departmental procedures, inspect your facilities, and review any other items that may be of concern.

### Preaward Survey Requirements

Figure 9-3 illustrates Standard Form 1403, Preaward Survey of Prospective Contractor (General). This form tells the survey team what is to be reviewed. Block 19 in Section III of the form lists five major factors for review: technical capability, production capability, quality assurance capability, financial capability, and accounting system. Block 20 lists other factors that may be specific to a program such as environment, transportation, packaging, security, and safety.

Each of the five major factors for review in Block 19 has its own form for recording the results of the review. Knowing what is on these forms will help you prepare for the survey and present the information in an efficient and understandable manner. You should request these forms

**PREAWARD SURVEY OF PROSPECTIVE CONTRACTOR (GENERAL)**

1. SERIAL NO. *(For surveying activity use)*

FORM APPROVED OMB NO. 3090-0110

**SECTION I – REQUEST** *(For Completion by Contracting Office)*

2. NAME AND ADDRESS OF SURVEYING ACTIVITY

3. SOLICITATION NO.

4. TOTAL OFFERED PRICE $

5. TYPE OF CONTRACT

6A. NAME AND ADDRESS OF SECONDARY SURVEY ACTIVITY *(For surveying activity use)*

7. NAME AND ADDRESS PROSPECTIVE CONTRACTOR

6B. TELEPHONE NO. *(Include autovon, Wats/FTS, if available)*

8. WILL CONTRACTING OFFICE PARTICIPATE IN SURVEY?
☐ YES ☐ NO

9. DATE OF THIS REQUEST

10. DATE REPORT REQUIRED

11. Prospective contractor represents that it ☐ is, ☐ is not a small business concern.

12. WALSH-HEALEY CONTRACTS ACT *(Check applicable box(es))*
A. IS NOT APPLICABLE
B. IS APPLICABLE AND PROSPECTIVE CONTRACTOR REPRESENTS HIS CLASSIFICATION AS:
☐ MANUFACTURER ☐ REGULAR DEALER
☐ OTHER *(Specify)*

13. NAME AND ADDRESS OF PARENT COMPANY *(If applicable)*

14. PLANT AND LOCATION *(If different from Item 7, above)*

15A. NAME OF REQUESTING ACTIVITY CONTRACTING OFFICER

15B. SIGNATURE

15C. TELEPHONE NO. *(Include autovon, Wats/FTS, if available)*

16A. NAME AND ADDRESS OF SECONDARY REQUESTING ACTIVITY *(For surveying authority use)*

16B. TELEPHONE NO. *(Include autovon, Wats/FTS, if available)*

17. FIRM'S CONTACT FOR SURVEY

A. NAME AND TITLE

B. TELEPHONE NO. *(Include Area Code)*

**SECTION II – DATA** *(For Completion by Contracting Office)*

| 18A. ITEM NO. | 18B. NATIONAL STOCK NUMBER (NEW) AND NOMENCLATURE | | 18C. TOTAL QUANTITY | 18D. UNIT PRICE | 18E. DELIVERY SCHEDULE (a) | (b) | (c) | (d) | (e) |
|---|---|---|---|---|---|---|---|---|---|
| | | SOLICITED | | | | | | | |
| | | OFFERED | | $ | | | | | |
| | | SOLICITED | | | | | | | |
| | | OFFERED | | $ | | | | | |
| | | SOLICITED | | | | | | | |
| | | OFFERED | | $ | | | | | |
| | | SOLICITED | | | | | | | |
| | | OFFERED | | $ | | | | | |
| | | SOLICITED | | | | | | | |
| | | OFFERED | | $ | | | | | |
| | | SOLICITED | | | | | | | |
| | | OFFERED | | $ | | | | | |
| | | SOLICITED | | | | | | | |
| | | OFFERED | | $ | | | | | |
| | | SOLICITED | | | | | | | |
| | | OFFERED | | $ | | | | | |
| | | SOLICITED | | | | | | | |
| | | OFFERED | | $ | | | | | |

NSN 7540-01-140-5525 1403-101 STANDARD FORM 1403 (10-83)
Prescribed by GSA
FAR (48 CFR) 53.209-1(a)

**Figure 9-3.** Preaward Survey of Prospective Contractor (SF 1403) used by the survey team to evaluate the bidder.

**SECTION III – FACTORS TO BE INVESTIGATED**

Column (a) is for request. Columns (b) and (c) are for survey results. Provide a narrative explanation substantiating each factor for which Column (b) or (c) is checked.

| 19. MAJOR FACTORS | CHK. (a) | SAT. (b) | UN-SAT. (c) | 20. OTHER FACTORS *(Provide specific requirements in Remarks)* | CHK. (a) | SAT. (b) | UN-SAT. (c) |
|---|---|---|---|---|---|---|---|
| A. TECHNICAL CAPABILITY | | | | A. GOVERNMENT PROPERTY CONTROL | | | |
| B. PRODUCTION CAPABILITY | | | | B. TRANSPORTATION | | | |
| C. QUALITY ASSURANCE CAPABILITY | | | | C. PACKAGING | | | |
| D. FINANCIAL CAPABILITY | | | | D. SECURITY | | | |
| E. ACCOUNTING SYSTEM | | | | E. PLANT SAFETY | | | |
| 21. IS THIS A SHORT FORM PREAWARD REPORT? | | | | F. ENVIRONMENTAL/ENERGY CONSIDERATIONS | | | |
| ☐ YES ☐ NO | | | | G. OTHER *(Specify)* | | | |

22. IS A FINANCIAL ASSISTANCE PAYMENT PROVISION IN THE SOLICITATION?

☐ YES ☐ NO

23. REMARKS

**SECTION IV – SURVEYING ACTIVITY RECOMMENDATIONS**

| 24. RECOMMEND | 25A. NAME AND TITLE OF SURVEY APPROVING OFFICIAL | 25B. TELEPHONE NO. |
|---|---|---|
| ☐ A. COMPLETE AWARD<br>☐ B. PARTIAL AWARD<br>*(Quantity* ________<br>☐ C. NO AWARD | 25C. SIGNATURE | 25D. DATE |

STANDARD FORM 1403 BACK (10-83)

**Figure 9-3.** (*Continued*)

from the contracting officer prior to the survey. Some of the more important review factors on each form are highlighted below:

SF 1404, Preaward Survey of Prospective Contractor—Technical

- A list of key personnel giving names, qualifications, experience, and length of service with the prospective contractor.
- A narrative evaluation of the technical capabilities as they relate to the requirements.
- A description of any technical capabilities that the prospective contractor lacks, and what is proposed to obtain these technical capabilities.
- A series of questions regarding your understanding of specifications, drawings, exhibits, and technical data requirements.
- A recommendation to make a complete award, partial award, or no award.

SF 1405, Preaward Survey of Prospective Contractor—Production

- A description of your plant facilities.
- The square footage of your manufacturing and storage areas and the space available for the product being purchased. This also includes blocks for indicating whether this space is adequate or inadequate.
- Miscellaneous plant observations such as housekeeping, adequate power and fuel supply sources, material handling equipment, transportation facilities, etc.
- A listing of manufacturing, special tooling, and test equipment. The government will review the quantity on hand, quantity required, condition, and source of equipment if not on hand.
- A description of parts, materials, and subcontracts with the longest lead time or relating to crucial items.
- A personnel section that categorizes the number of skilled and unskilled production workers and engineering and administrative personnel on board, how many additional personnel in each category are required for the job, and if they are available.
- A narrative description of your delivery performance record.
- A listing of related previous government projects.
- A listing of current government and civilian projects scheduled for the next 10 months.

- A narrative description of the relationship between management, production, and inspection departments.
- A narrative description and evaluation of your production control system.

SF 1406, Preaward Survey of Prospective Contractor—Quality Assurance

- A narrative description of the quality assurance organization.
- A listing of prospective contractor quality assurance officials and years of quality assurance experience.
- A questionnaire on whether identical or similar items have been produced or serviced.
- A series of questions on the number of quality personnel; the contractors understanding of the quality requirements; the existence and proper functioning of methods for inspection, test, and calibration; and the existence of a system for identifying and processing nonconforming material, etc.
- A recommendation to award or not award the contract.

SF 1407, Preaward Survey of Prospective Contractor—Financial Capability

- General information on the type of company (proprietorship, partnership, corporation).
- Records of the latest balance sheet and profit and loss statement. This includes ratios of current assets to current liabilities, acid test, and total liabilities to net worth.
- How the contractor finances its operations. Do you use your own assets, bank credit, or other means?
- Will the contractor be requesting government financial aid through progress payments or a guaranteed loan? A record of any existing government financial aid being received.
- A narrative description of the prospective contractors business and financial reputation. This includes references from your bank, trade creditors, and commercial financial services or credit organizations.
- A record of projected sales for the next six quarters, both current and anticipated.

SF 1408, Preaward Survey of Prospective Contractor—Accounting System

- Is your accounting system in accord with generally accepted accounting principles?
- Does your accounting system provide for the normal business functions such as direct and indirect cost segregation, timekeeping, labor distribution, job costing, etc.?
- Does your accounting system provide financial information to support contractual requirements such as progress payments?
- Is your accounting system designed to develop accurate data for use in pricing follow-on acquisitions?
- Is your accounting system currently in full operation?

## Preparing for a Preaward Survey

As you can tell by the above description of the preaward survey forms, your staff is going to be very busy. The preaward survey is your opportunity to sell your company and personnel to the government. You want the survey team to leave your business feeling warm and fuzzy from head to toe. How do you accomplish this? By having all your ducks in a row.

First, you should know that the government is very strict about the acceptance of favors or gratuities by government employees. Therefore, don't offer to buy lunch or hand out company-sponsored souvenirs. Your business should function strictly as it would on a regular daily basis. With this in mind, develop a plan for marketing your product, facilities, and personnel that accomplishes the objective of answering the survey forms. Listed below are some tips for conducting a successful preaward survey.

- Be sure your housekeeping is in order. All desks should look neat and free of clutter. All manufacturing areas should be free of trash and easily accessible. Don't leave things sitting in aisles for people to walk around.
- Assemble a staff of personnel who know your operations from front door to back door. They will be used for tour guides. Plan what items or areas of interest you particularly want to emphasize and be sure your guides know this and know what to say. These tours are an excellent opportunity to instill confidence of your capabilities in the survey team. If you are the best at something, tell them. Be sure to also tell them why you are the best.

- Review your procedures. If they haven't been updated to reflect current practices do so before the survey. Be sure the procedures are understandable, easy to read, and neat. Don't present procedures for review that have words crossed out or writing in the margins.
- Be sure you have personnel available that are familiar with the procedures and can answer questions that may arise.
- Review any government standards or specifications that you are unfamiliar with to gain a basic knowledge of them. This will help you answer questions specific to government contracting.
- If you have produced or are presently producing like or similar equipment, have a sample or samples available for the government to look at.
- Have an area available for the survey team to work in. It should be equipped with a telephone. Also be sure the area is quiet and that the team will be free from interruption.

# 10
# After the Sale

Winning a government contract is something like winning the lottery.

First the government must confirm that you have the winning numbers. Next, the government must confirm your identification. Then the media will announce that you have won millions of dollars. And, just like the lottery, you will not get those millions in one lump sum but in several installments over a set amount of time. Also, it is highly probable that someone will appear from out of nowhere claiming to have the same numbers and wanting a piece of the pie. You will have to contend with those who now know that you are the victor and want to attach themselves to your winnings in some form or another.

This chapter is designed to help you get off the ground and on your way to becoming successful as a government contractor.

## Launching the New Contract

The time immediately after contract award is a very busy one. There are many things that have to be done and done quickly.

There are staffing needs to fill and schedules to prepare. Vendors and subcontractors must be decided upon and brought on board. Conferences must be arranged and conducted. Administrative matters need to be attended to.

It is very important for your company to get this project off the ground smoothly. This will build the government's confidence in your abilities. The clock is ticking and you are the timekeeper.

## First Things First

Aside from staffing and schedules there are a few things that will need your immediate attention.

Take a few minutes and read the contract. You should be extremely familiar with the clauses, representations, and certifications by now.

Make a list of all the questions you have that are unanswered.

Write down what you believe to be the important milestones and delivery dates.

You will need to know the names, addresses, and telephone numbers of key government officials who will be working with you on this contract. Among these officials should be the contracting officer, the administrative contracting officer (sometimes assigned to help the contracting officer administer the contract), and the accounting office responsible for paying you.

If you are manufacturing a product you will need to coordinate the official item nomenclature, national stock number, model number assignment, and serial number assignment with the government.

If the contract provides for government furnished equipment, you will have to request it.

You will also need to be sure that any government required security clearances are in order. There may be parts of the contract that are not available until you have "top secret" clearance.

Then there is the matter of scheduling the use of any equipment or facilities other than your own, whether they be owned by the government or by private industry. Government test facilities may be booked up a year or more in advance.

## The Postaward Conference

The contracting officer may schedule a postaward conference if the government or contractor asks for it. It should be noted that there will not always be a postaward conference. If you feel the need for one, write to the contracting officer and request it as soon after contract award as possible.

The purpose of the postaward conference is to review all contractual requirements and come to a mutual understanding of them. This is the time to go through your checklist of unanswered questions and pose them to the responsible government representatives who can get you an answer.

The contracting officer will establish a time and place for the conference, usually at your facility. The contracting officer will also prepare an agenda and arrange for the attendance of government representatives.

Government attendees at the postaward conference usually include the contracting officer, program manager, project engineer, quality control representative, and administrative contracting officer. You will also find assorted personnel from engineering, testing, logistics and other data disciplines, reliability, maintainability, and safety.

The number and type of people who attend the conference depend upon the complexity of the contract, the results of the preaward survey, and your performance history or experience in the goods or services being produced.

**The Golden Rule.** The postaward conference is chaired by the contracting officer. That person will usually begin the conference by introducing the government representatives and asking you to introduce your personnel. The next thing you will hear is a statement that goes something like this:

> Nothing said during this meeting is to be acted upon by the contractor, or interpreted as redirection of the contract, unless it is recorded in writing and incorporated into the contract by the contracting officer.

This is the golden rule of government contracting. Pay close attention to these words. Invariably throughout the course of the contract you will receive direction by someone other than the contracting officer about something that changes the contract. At that point you should immediately request that it be put in writing by the contracting officer. Do not expose yourself to a conflict and possible litigation because a government representative usurps the contracting officer's authority. At the very least telephone the contracting officer, inform him or her of the incident, and confirm that new direction will follow in writing.

The actual conduct of the conference is fairly routine. The contracting officer will go through each section of the contract and ask if the contractor has any questions. The government will also confirm your certifications and representations, as well as the delivery schedule. The next material to be reviewed will be any attachments, statements of work, and contract data requirements lists. Again you will have the opportunity to ask questions.

Once all the material in the contract and its supporting documents have been reviewed, there will be a recap to confirm any action items generated from the meeting. Dates should be set for initiating these actions. The meeting will then be adjourned.

## Preparing for the Postaward Conference

As stated above, the postaward conference should be held as soon as possible after contract award. This is done for two reasons:

First, it is a good idea to receive clarification while all the contract requirements and all your questions are fresh in your mind, and before any work has been performed.

Second, now is the time to meet the people you are going to work with and establish a personal association with them. Government contracts often last for extended periods of time. It helps both parties to be able to associate a face and personality with a name that comes on a letter or a voice heard on the telephone.

Once you know who the government attendees are, plan to have members of your staff or subcontractor personnel who are their counterparts attend the conference. It would be advantageous to meet with these people prior to the conference to discuss any questions you might ask, and any answers you may have for questions anticipated from the government. Now is the time to request schedule dates for other conferences or ask how you are to bill for something and when you are to bill for it. This is also the time to request any changes to the contract that you feel are necessary or justifiable.

**Recording the Postaward Conference.** At any government meeting it is extremely important to keep good records of the proceedings. You may be required by contract to do so. If not, you should do so for your own benefit. A good stenographer can usually keep up with what is being discussed. Keep in mind that some of the information may be of a technical nature and it would benefit the person keeping records to sit by someone familiar with the requirements.

An alternate method for keeping records is to tape record the meeting. This way you know exactly what has been said. It requires more expense on your part, and the government may not be happy with the arrangement, but I have attended several meetings where this method was used.

I have also attended meetings where an official court reporter was used to record the proceedings. However, this was a case where discussions in previous meetings had been misinterpreted or denied by one or both parties. Court reporters have a way of making people feel uneasy as they record every "uh" and "ah" that is said. When people feel uneasy there is the potential for minor misunderstandings to become major conflicts. This is not what you want when working with the government.

Once the conference is concluded, the person responsible for preparing the minutes submits them to the contracting officer for review and approval. The contracting officer will usually circulate the minutes to the attendees, both government and contractor, for concurrence. When the minutes become finalized they are incorporated into the contract via a contract modification. Then and only then do any modifications discussed become contractual and can they be acted upon.

**Action Item Form.** Develop a form that can be used to record and to follow up any actions to be taken as a result of the postaward conference. Figure 10-1 illustrates a sample action item form.

The whole purpose of an action item form is to describe what needs to be done, when it needs to be done, and who is supposed to do it. This could be where you take note, for instance, that a paragraph in the statement of work is worded incorrectly. The action form could record the fact that the contracting officer is supposed to go back and correct the paragraph by a certain date.

When preparing an action item, be sure that all the parties involved understand what action is to accomplished. Also be sure that the dates for accomplishing the work are realistic yet in line with any schedule constraints. You need to allow appropriate time for the action items, but you also need to have the results in time for any task contingent on the action item.

**Gratuities.** Remember that the government is not allowed to take anything from a contractor free of charge. This is clearly stated in the FAR and should be scrupulously adhered to.

You would be surprised though, at how many coffee mugs or tee shirts bearing the name of the program or product being produced will be purchased for a minimal price. The government is just as proud of this program as you are, and wants it to be a success just as much as you do.

**A Final Word.** You are now the successful bidder and the contract is yours. Use the postaward conference as a springboard to build on relationships and to build the government's confidence in what you can do. Always offer tours for people who have not been to your facility before. Just like any sales operation, the longer you keep your client's attention the better your chances are of making the sale. Subtle references to your capabilities at opportune times will help people remember who you are and what you do. But be careful not to overdo it.

ACTION ITEM FORM

DATE: ____________________

PERSON/AGENCY REQUESTING: ____________________

CONTRACT REFERENCE: ____________________

ACTION ITEM REQUEST: ____________________

ACTION ITEM RESPONSIBILITY: ____________________

SUSPENSE DATE: ____________________

ACTION TAKEN: ____________________

ACTION ITEM COMPLETED BY: ________ DATE: ________

**Figure 10-1.** Sample action item form.

## Guidance Conferences

Most likely there are other conferences or reviews required by the contract that should occur shortly after award. These conferences are usually called "guidance conferences" of one sort or another. Some examples are the provisioning guidance conference, the training guidance conference, and the logistics guidance conference.

Review these conference requirements and make an assessment of whether they can be held in conjunction or concurrently with each other or with the postaward conference. Once you have done this, ask the contracting officer to schedule these conferences.

**Location.** The conference may take place at your facility or at a government facility, so this may have some bearing on whether they can be scheduled with other conferences. Also when the conferences deal with something of a technical nature, such as provisioning parts for supply support, there may be a multitude of government personnel that wish to attend. Therefore, in all likelihood guidance conferences will be conducted at a government facility and require your staff to travel.

**Attendees.** Send the person responsible for this effort, supporting staff if necessary, your contract administrator, and a representative from your subcontractor if they play a major role in this effort. This means you should send two to four people only.

How many government people will attend? I have seen upwards of 25 people in attendance. At these meetings, I have found that three or four will do most of the talking, while the others sit and listen, and even sleep.

**Conducting the Guidance Conference.** Be sure first of all to establish who the leader of your group is. This should be the person responsible for the effort you are receiving guidance on.

Next, seek out the government leader and quickly establish a good rapport. This will help when the person sitting at the back of the room, who has been silent for the last six hours, decides they want to require you to do something ridiculous that is beyond the scope of the contract. Perhaps they have decided they want to conduct two training classes for 15 students each instead of one training class for 30 students, which was the original contract requirement. You will incur additional expense if you agree to do this. Be sure to let the government leader know that you will be happy to do this but it is not what was originally ordered and the extra cost to do so will have to be added to the contract.

Guidance conferences cover specific details of a contract requirement, sometimes to the nth degree. Be prepared to ask any questions you may have as well as to listen to government representatives expound on their knowledge of the subject.

Be a patient listener. These are the people who are going to review your work and recommend approval or disapproval to the contracting officer. Keep good records of the proceedings, and be sure they are incorporated into the contract before you act on them.

## Staffing Your New Program

By now you should have in mind who you want to assign to work on this job and what their qualifications are. You also know the resources required in the areas of purchasing, accounting, manufacturing, and quality control. However, some company positions found in government contracting are not common in the commercial world. The positions of contract administrator and program manager are peculiar to government contract work.

### Contract Administrator

The contract administrator is responsible for keeping all the paperwork flowing. This is a major responsibility in a government contract. Among the duties of the contract administrator are:

- Conduct all written and oral communication regarding contractual matters, with the contracting officer or the administrative contracting officer
- Monitor contract deliverables for timeliness of submission and report any delays to executive management
- Coordinate the billing and receipt of funds for all contract line items
- Interpret the FARs as they apply to the contract
- Coordinate the review, approval or disapproval, negotiation, and incorporation of any changes to the contract
- Report contract status to the government and executive management
- Participate in any meetings with the government to review contractual issues

### Program Manager

The program manager is responsible for the daily activities of the program. The duties of the program manager include:

- Monitor the daily progress of the program, identify potential problems, determine their resolution, and inform executive management of program status
- Identify resource requirements and participate through direct or indirect supervision in the research, design, development, and testing of the good or service being produced

- Monitor the program budget and take necessary actions to keep it in balance
- Develop, monitor, and update the program schedule
- Oversee subcontract activities
- Coordinate program management activities with the government program manager
- Participate in any meeting with the government to review program issues
- Monitor contract deliverables and coordinate submissions and billings with the contract administrator
- Coordinate or prepare written communication regarding program issues with the contract administrator
- Prepare and review contract changes, and make recommendation for approval or disapproval

## Support Staff

The contract administrator and program manager are the two most important positions within your firm that deal with the government. However, the support staff entrusted with a majority of the work will make your effort successful. You are already familiar with many of these job titles, but some may be new to you. In any event, a recap of these positions and their responsibilities may help you with your resource planning.

**Project and Design Engineers.** The engineering staff will need direction in the research, design, and development of the good or service being produced. While the overall responsibility for this rests with the program manager, the manager's time is quickly consumed and he or she needs to be able to rely on someone to take up the slack and keep the effort progressing. The project engineer is tasked with this responsibility. This individual will supervise a team of design engineers in the evolution and documentation of your product.

**Test Engineer.** If your contract requires testing of the product or service you may want to assign a test engineer. Some test efforts are minimal and would not dictate the need for this position. Other test efforts are large scale requiring several test technicians, a variety of test and measurement equipment, facilities planning, consumables, and logistics planning. A test engineer can relieve a lot of headaches for the program manager and the company as well.

**Data Manager.** If your contract has a host of contract data requirements lists (CDRLs), you will want to assign a data manager to this effort. The government has increased the demand for analyses and reports to be used in identifying the support needs of the products they purchase once they are placed in service. This data takes the form of technical manuals, provisioning technical documentation, logistics support analysis, reliability, maintainability, safety, and human factors analysis and predictions.

All of these reports require someone to initiate the research and documentation of the various elements involved from a wide variety of sources. These include engineering personnel, part suppliers, government sources, and maybe even the mailman. If your requirements go much beyond an operation and service manual, it is best to empower someone to coordinate these documentation efforts. Don't be fooled into thinking that your program manager or project engineer has the time to pool all this information and make it presentable to the government at the required delivery times and in the required format.

**Configuration Manager.** If your contract is a design and development program, your product will be in constant evolution. Once the product has an established baseline, usually when the government has approved it for production, you need to record this change to document the whys and wherefores of the finished product. This information supports future efforts to operate and maintain the equipment once it is placed into service. The configuration manager has the job of keeping up with and recording all of these changes.

## Preparing the Program Schedule

The program schedule will become your roadmap for executing the contract delivery requirements on time. It should identify all milestones, tasks required to achieve each milestone, and subtasks required to achieve each task. It will also identify resources and estimated time for each task or subtask. Just as you must first start your car and pull out of the driveway heading south to reach First Street; you must first develop a topical outline, then instructor and student handbooks, and present a training course on how to operate and maintain your soft-serve ice cream machine.

The program schedule is best accomplished by preparing a PERT chart and identifying the critical path, as we discussed in Chapter 5. The key to developing a good schedule is to identify the entire work effort and allocate resources and time to it as accurately as you can.

Let's take a closer look at one of the tasks identified in Figure 5-3, assembling the first article unit. Figure 10-2 will help with this analysis. We will keep our example simple. Assembling the first article unit is a task of achieving the milestone "submit first article test report." What are the subtasks involved in assembling the first article unit? What resources are required? How much time is required?

| Task/ subtask | Description | Resource | Time (hrs) |
|---|---|---|---|
| 001 | Assemble first article | — | 7.25 |
| 001A | Make parts | — | 1.65 |
| 001AA | Determine make or buy | Engineering | 0.03 |
| 001AB | I.D. raw matl reqts | Engineering | 0.03 |
| 001AC | Source suppliers | Purchasing | 0.08 |
| 001AD | Negotiate purchase | Purchasing | 0.08 |
| 001AE | Issue purchase order | Purchasing | 0.50 |
| 001AE01 | Compare prices | Purchasing | 0.08 |
| 001AE02 | Confirm availability | Purchasing | 0.03 |
| 001AE03 | Certify supplier | Purchasing | 0.08 |
| 001AE04 | Prepare purchase order | Purchasing | 0.17 |
| 001AE05 | Get purchase order approval | Purchasing | 0.08 |
| 001AE06 | Mail purchase order | Purchasing | 0.05 |
| 001AF | Receive material | Materials | 0.25 |
| 001AG | Inspect material | Quality | 0.17 |
| 001AH | Transfer material to work in process | Materials | 0.17 |
| 001AI | Make part | Manufacturing | 0.25 |
| 001AJ | Inspect parts | Quality | 0.08 |
| 001B | Purchase parts | Purchasing | 1.10 |
| 001C | Assemble subassemblies | Manufacturing | 4.00 |
| 001D | Inspect | Quality | 0.50 |

**Figure 10-2.** Sample task analysis.

Assuming that you already have a drawing package, the tasks required to assemble the first article unit are:

1. Make parts
2. Purchase parts
3. Assemble subassemblies

The subtasks required of the task "make parts" are:

1. Identify raw material requirements
2. Source suppliers
3. Negotiate purchase
4. Issue purchase order
5. Receive material
6. Inspect material
7. Transfer material to work station
8. Make part
9. Inspect part

The subtasks required of the task "issue purchase order" are:

1. Compare prices
2. Confirm availability
3. Certify supplier
4. Prepare purchase order
5. Get purchase order approval
6. Mail purchase order

Next let's assign resources and estimate the time involved to make parts. The subtasks of issuing the purchase order can all be accomplished by the purchasing agent at an estimated time of 0.5 hours. The subtasks of "make parts" can be accomplished by various personnel in 1.65 hours, which includes 0.5 hours to issue the purchase order. The subtasks to assemble a first article unit can be accomplished in 7.25 hours by various personnel. Obviously, this is a very simple piece of equipment with very few parts. Imagine identifying the tasks and subtasks required to produce a Stealth Fighter.

The assignment of task/subtask numbers shown in Figure 10-2 is helpful in linking subtasks to tasks, particularly if you are only viewing a portion of the schedule. It also helps in tracking the budget through the various departments. There are a variety of ways to assign this number so feel free to use whatever system works best for you.

As you can see, developing and monitoring the program schedule can be a full-time job. There are a number of software programs available that can make this job easier. The software will track time, resources, budget, task linkage, and critical path and allow you to adjust for accelerations or delays. Investing in a program management software package is money well spent.

## Renegotiating with Vendors

Vendor renegotiation may be a touchy subject. Nevertheless, it is worth consideration. If you have gone into the bid with a supplier who has given you an indication that they might be able to reduce the price if they were sure of the business, now is the time to drop the hammer. After all, you are in the driver's seat and they know it. There is no more playing one bidder against another. If you don't go with their product, they are a loser.

On the other hand, if a supplier has been completely up front with you and indicated they have given you their best price, and you feel this to be true, close the deal. You don't want to enter into a long contract with the government and have to fight a supplier for the duration. You never know when the government may come to you and ask to expedite delivery and increase order quantity. A good working relationship with your supplier may mean the difference in being able to do this.

## Awarding Subcontracts

### When to Subcontract

If you are purchasing doorstops for 1000 units at a penny apiece, a purchase order will generally suffice. If you are purchasing a component subassembly for 1000 units that comprises 30 percent of your total unit cost, you will want to develop a subcontract.

Where you draw the line between a general purchase order and a subcontract is purely judgmental. While there are a host of reasons for using a subcontract, basically you should ask yourself what is the supplier's involvement in the contract, and what is the impact if they fail to perform.

Here are some questions to help you decide whether to issue a subcontract:

- What is the supplier's past history and what is your relationship with them? Do they or have they delivered on time? Have you used them successfully before?
- What is the aggregate cost of their goods or services in relation to the contract cost? As our example above indicates, you will want more control over some suppliers than others.
- What is the availability of the good or service from other suppliers and what is the cost? If your supplier should become unable to deliver or if you should decide to terminate your agreement, how quickly and at what cost can you replace that supplier?
- Are you required by the contract to award subcontracts? Depending on the dollar value of the contract, you may be required to do this.
- What impact does the supplier's participation have on your ability to successfully fulfill your contractual obligations? If the supplier is responsible for designing some new state of the art equipment detailed by you in your proposal, and this was a contributing factor to your receiving the award, you want to be sure they deliver or pay the price for default.
- Did the supplier commit to support the good or service as a part of the original quotation at no additional cost? If you are buying an engine and the government requires an overhaul manual, you don't want to put yourself in the position of having a misunderstanding about supplying the manual or what it will cost. You also want to obtain a copyright release for printing purposes.

## What to Include in a Subcontract

The format for a subcontract does not have to be as formal as your contract. It should however contain enough information to ensure performance, and protect against nonperformance. All that may be required is a simple statement of work that details what the supplier is supposed to do and incorporates all of your contract by reference and attachment of those applicable portions.

What should be included in a subcontract depends on what is being subcontracted. The subcontract can be sectioned into the clauses and the statement of work. Two other important parts of the subcontract are the work schedule and the invoicing schedule. The schedules should be referenced in the subcontract and included in the purchase order. This will allow you to make adjustments to either by revising the purchase order. This is a little easier than amending the subcontract.

Review your contract to determine which clauses you want to incorporate into the subcontract. Some will be obvious. If the government requires you to conform to the Americans with Disabilities Act, you need to require your subcontractor to do likewise. If you have any doubts about whether or not to include a clause, include it.

## Preparing the Subcontract Statement of Work

The subcontract statement of work is prepared in much the same way as your statement of work from the government. You need to pass on all the requirements that the government has imposed on you as they relate to the subcontractor's effort. Consider the following when preparing the statement of work:

- Pass on all performance requirements. Pay particular attention to reliability, maintainability, safety, and human factors. You may want to impose different requirements on your subcontractor in these areas. Review your total product to see how the subcontractor's part affects the net requirement.
- Include provision for support in other areas. If you are going to need help in training government personnel, field service assistance, or participating in government reviews, put it in writing.
- Be sure to cover all the little details. How will their part be packaged? How will it be shipped? Who pays for the shipping?
- Establish a system to communicate changes. There will be changes in the contract and in your design efforts. Be sure your system provides a means for informing the subcontractor and receiving confirmation from the subcontractor.
- Include provisions for you and the government to visit the subcontractor's facilities. The government should be allowed to do this only with your permission and when accompanied by a representative of your firm.
- Establish a key contact within the subcontractor organization who will be responsible for the work effort and has the authority to make things happen.

- Establish a reporting system that documents progress, delays, and resolutions. This will come in handy when its time to pay.
- If key personnel qualifications or security clearances are an important part of your contract, pass them on. You don't want the government to stop your test effort because your subcontracted test manager has nine years of experience and "secret clearance" when the contract calls for ten years experience and "top secret clearance."

### Preparing the Subcontract Purchase Order

The subcontract purchase order will probably not be much different from any other purchase order. It should have all the usual terms and conditions. In addition, it should include a delivery schedule that allows you adequate time to perform your work once you receive the good or service from the subcontractor. If the subcontractor manufactures a part, allow time for your assembly efforts. If the subcontractor supplies a report, allow time for review and revision.

Keep in mind that if you have a work task that drives the subcontractor's task, you will have to plan accordingly. Don't penalize the subcontractor because you didn't deliver the drawing for his part on time.

The purchase order should also include an invoicing schedule. This schedule should be based progressively on work performed by the subcontractor. You may want to hold back part of the payment until you receive government approval of the work. You will certainly want to include a penalty provision for late delivery.

## Contract Changes

Surely you have been living with something in the contract that just doesn't seem right. It may be a communication problem. The language in a clause may be incorrect. It may be a performance problem. Perhaps, when you run through the math, 2 + 2 = 9. Or there may be an error in the delivery schedule or the method for invoicing.

Whatever it is, don't be afraid to call it to the attention of the contracting officer. You may want to telephone first and later follow up in writing. To get this approval, you should:

1. Address the issue in detail, telling why you think it needs to be changed

2. Describe any impact the change has on other parts of the contract
3. Prepare your proposed change exactly as you want it to appear in the contract
4. Describe any benefits of the change to you and the government
5. If a change in the contract results in a price increase or decrease, provide a detailed breakdown
6. Indicate a time needed for approval of the change

Keep in mind that you and the government are a team now and you both have a common goal of producing the best product at the most economical price. If a contract change helps to accomplish this goal, the government will be receptive to it. It may take a while to get it approved because you are dealing with the largest bureaucracy in the world. But then again, Rome wasn't built in a day.

Contract changes will come in the form of a contract modification. This is written confirmation signed by the contracting officer to proceed with the change. You may or may not be required to sign the document concurring with the change. Be sure to read all contract modifications carefully and have them reviewed by the staff members who will be charged with carrying out the change.

A word of caution on requesting a contract change. Do *not* bid a job expecting to get approval of a contract change after award. You must clear up any major changes prior to bidding. Always bid the requirements as they are spelled out in the bid document. To do otherwise, such as bidding with the idea that the government will go along with your proposed change, could spell disaster. It is easier to convince the government to take money out of a contract because the scope of work has decreased than it is to get them to put money in because of an increase in requirements.

## If at First You Don't Succeed

We have said from the very outset that the business of being a government supplier is highly competitive. We have also said that if you are truly serious about becoming a government supplier, and if you do you homework, you stand just as much chance as the next person in carving your niche in a multibillion dollar market. This book is designed to help you gain an advantage over your competitors. However, past experience has proved that you can do everything within your power that is possible and still come up short. If this should happen, don't be discouraged.

Believe it or not the government has been known to make a decision and then reverse it. If you do not win when you make a bid, there are two alternative courses of action. One is relatively simple and should always be taken. The other can result in a long, drawn-out affair, possibly involving litigation, and should be approached after careful thought.

## Debriefings

When a contract is awarded on a basis other than price alone, you have the right to submit a written request for a debriefing. The government is obligated to provide you with its basis for the selection decision and contract award. The government will also provide you with an evaluation of your proposal identifying significant weak or deficient factors. You should always request a debriefing in order to improve your communication skills the next time around.

If you view the debriefing as constructive criticism, you can learn from it. If you request the debriefing to find out about your competition, you will come away from the table empty handed. The government is *not* required to provide the following in the debriefing:

- Point by point comparisons between your proposal and other offerors' proposals
- The relative merits or technical standing of competitors
- The evaluation scoring
- Any information that is not releasable under the Freedom of Information Act

## Protests

Any offeror who feels they have an objection to an award has the right to file a written protest. You should know this for two reasons. First, you may want to file a protest if you do not win and have an objection. Second, chances are that you will be protested against if you do win.

The FAR, 42 CFR 33.101, defines protest as

> a written objection by an interested party to a solicitation by an agency for offers for a proposed contract for the acquisition of sup-

> plier or services or a written objection by an interested party to a proposed award of the award of such a contract.

The FAR also defines an interested party as

> an actual or prospective offeror whose direct economic interest would be affected by the award of a contract or by the failure to award a contract.

Protests may be filed in writing before or after award to any of the following, preferably in this order:

1. The contracting officer of the agency that solicited the good or service
2. The General Accounting Office (GAO)
3. The General Services Board of Contract Appeals (GSBCA)

There are specific rules for filing each kind of protest, which the FAR details.

When a protest is filed it generally holds up award of the contract until a determination is made. If you are the protester, that's fine. If you are the successful bidder, this may cause problems. If you are an offeror neither protesting nor being protested against, you will probably be asked to extend your bid acceptance date.

Since most protests are filed with the agency first, you should be aware that the FAR prohibits award until the matter is resolved unless the contracting officer first determines that one of the following applies:

- The supplies or services to be contracted for are urgently required.
- Delivery or performance will be unduly delayed by failure to make award promptly.
- A prompt award will otherwise be advantageous to the government.

Therefore, if you are the victim of a protest, be sure to find out how badly the good or service is needed, and be sure to point out how delivery will be delayed if the protest is not cleared up quickly.

Filing a protest can work to your advantage if you really feel you have an objection that the government will rule for in your favor.

For example, let's say you have been manufacturing soft-serve ice cream machines for 25 years and bid a job for 1000 units at $100 per unit ($100,000).

Stepfast Shoe Company, who has manufactured shoes for the past 25 years, decided to bid the 1000 units at $90 per unit ($90,000).

You have been notified that Stepfast is the low bidder and the government intends to award. You should probably file a protest pointing out that you clearly have the experience and the equipment, while it is most likely that Stepfast has no experience and will have to purchase equipment, which may cause delays in the program and possible default.

Does the government really want to pursue business with Stepfast for a $10,000 savings? I would hope not, and you have a chance, at least, that the government will agree once you point out the real differences between the two bids.

That's the best-case scenario. There are also a couple of reasons you may *not* want to file a protest.

First, protests can end up being a big expense in time and money. Second, they can also end up with no apparent winner.

Protests can result in the government deciding not to award to anyone and putting the good or service back out for bid again. Companies have spent thousands of dollars in legal fees and hundreds of hours to find out that they have to go back to square one of the bidding process if they want to win the award they should have won in the first place.

Before you file a protest, be sure you have a legitimate objection that you can convincingly present to the government.

# Sources for Additional Information

## Selected Government Purchasing Offices

Community Services
Administration
Procurement Division
1200 19th Street, NW
Washington, DC 20506

District of Columbia Government
Bureau of Materiel Management
Department of General Services
613 G Street NW
Washington, DC 20001

Defense Logistics Agency
Commander, Defense Personnel
Support Center
2800 South 20th Street
Philadelphia, PA 19101

Department of Health and Human
Services
Division of Contract and
Operations
Office of Management Services
Office of the Secretary
200 Independence Avenue, SW,
Room 443-H SP
Washington, DC 20201

Federal Communications
Commission
Procurement Branch
Room 326, Brown Building
1200 19th Street NW
Washington, DC 20554

Federal Energy Administration
Washington, DC 20461

Federal Highway Administration
Department of Transportation
400 7th Street, SW
Washington, DC 20590

National Aeronautics and Space
Administration
Kennedy Space Center, FL 32899

Panama Canal Company
Chief, Procurement Division
4400 Dauphine Street
New Orleans, LA 70140

Smithsonian Institution
Office of Supply Services
955 L'Enfant Plaza SW, Suite 3120
Washington, DC 20024

Social Security Administration
Division of Contracting and Procurement
P.O. Box 7696
Baltimore, MD 21207

Tennessee Valley Authority
Division of Purchasing
Chattanooga, TN 37401

U.S. Army Corps of Engineers
Office of Chief of Engineers
Department of the Army
Washington, DC 20314

U.S. Coast Guard
Chief, Procurement Division
2100 Second Street, SW
Washington, DC 20593

U.S. Department of Agriculture
Office of Operations, Procurement Division
Room 1567, South Building
Washington, DC 20250

U.S. Department of Commerce
Office of Procurement and Federal Assistance
Room 6855 HCHB
Washington, DC 20230

U.S. Department of Education
Assistance Management and Procurement Service
400 Maryland Avenue, SW
Washington, DC 20202

U.S. Department of Energy
Director, Office of Procurement Operations
1000 Independence Avenue, NW
Washington, DC 20585

U.S. Department of Health and Human Services
Division of Contract and Grant Operations
Room 443-H SP
200 Independence Avenue, SW
Washington, DC 20201

U.S. Department of Housing and Urban Development
Office of Procurement and Contracts
451 7th Street, SW, Room 5260
Washington, DC 20410

U.S. Department of Interior
Office of Administrative Services
Procurement Office
18th and C Streets, NW
Washington, DC 20240

U.S. Department of Justice
Procurement and Contracts Staff
10th & Constitution Avenue, NW
Washington, DC 20530

U.S. Department of Labor
Office of Administrative Services
200 Constitution Avenue, NW
Washington, DC 20210

U.S. Department of State
Office Supply Transportation Division and Procurement
Washington, DC 20520

U.S. Department of Transportation
Procurement Operations Division
Washington, DC 20590

U.S. Department of the Treasury
Internal Revenue Service
Contract and Procurement Branch
1111 Constitution Avenue NW, Room 1320
Washington, DC 20224

U.S. Environmental Protection Agency
Headquarters Contract Operations
Washington, DC 20460

U.S. Government Printing Office
North Capitol and H Streets, NW
Washington, DC 20401

U.S. Information Agency
Office of Contracts
Washington, DC 20547

U.S. Marine Corps Headquarters
Commandant of the Marine Corps
Department of the Navy
Washington, DC 20380

U.S. Nuclear Regulatory Commission
Division of Contracts
Washington, DC 20555

U.S. Postal Service
Office of Contracts
Procurement and Supply Dept.
475 L'Enfant Plaza SW
Washington, DC 20260

Veterans Administration
Office of Procurement & Supply
810 Vermont Avenue, NW
Washington, DC 20420

## General Services Administration Regional Offices

*Region 1: New England*

Business Service Center
General Services Administration
John W. McCormick Post Office and Courthouse
Boston, MA 02109

*Region 2: New York, New Jersey, Puerto Rico*

Business Service Center
General Services Administration
26 Federal Plaza
New York, NY 10007

*Region 3: Mid-Atlantic*

Business Service Center
General Services Administration
Ninth and Market Streets
Philadelphia, PA 19107

*Region 4: South*

Business Service Center
General Services Administration
1776 Peachtree Street, NW
Atlanta, GA 30309

*Region 5: Great Lakes*
Business Service Center
General Services Administration
230 South Dearborn Street
Chicago, IL 60604

*Region 6: Missouri Valley*
Business Service Center
General Services Administration
1500 East Bannister Road
Kansas City, MO 64131

*Region 7: Southwest*
Business Service Center
General Services Administration
819 Taylor Street
Fort Worth, TX 76102

*Region 8: Upper Midwest and Mountain*
Business Service Center
General Services Administration
Building 41
Denver Federal Center
Denver, CO 80225

*Region 9: California, Nevada, Hawaii*
Business Service Center
General Services Administration
525 Market Street
San Francisco, CA 94105

Business Service Center
General Services Administration
300 North Los Angeles Street
Los Angeles, CA. 90012

*Region 10: Northwest, Alaska*
Business Service Center
General Services Administration
440 Federal Building
915 Second Avenue
Seattle, WA 98174

## Purchasing Offices for Military Exchanges

Procurement Support Division
Army and Air Force Exchange Service
P.O. Box 22305
Dallas, TX 75222

Commanding Officer
Navy Resale and Support Office (AMD)
Fort Wadsworth
Staten Island, NY 10305

Marine Corps Exchange Service Headquarters
U.S. Marine Corps (LFE)
Washington, DC 20380

Commandant (FSU)
U.S. Coast Guard
400 7th Street, SW
Washington, DC 20590

## Purchasing Offices for Commissary Stores

Chief, Army Support Services
Department of the Army
Washington, DC 20315

Headquarters Air Force Commissary Service
HQAFCOMS
Kelly Air Force Base
San Antonio, TX 78241

Commanding Officer
Navy Resale and Support Office (AMD)
Fort Wadsworth
Staten Island, NY 10305

Marine Corps Exchange Service Headquarters
U.S. Marine Corps (LFE)
Washington, DC 20380

Commandant (FSU)
U.S. Coast Guard
400 7th Street SW
Washington, DC 20590

## Publications, Forms, and Specifications

*Code of Federal Regulations, Title 48*
Superintendent of Documents
Government Printing Office
Washington, DC 20402

*Commerce Business Daily*
Superintendent of Documents
Government Printing Office
Washington, DC 20402

*Contractors Paths to Grief*
Contact your local regional office of the Small Business Administration

*Doing Business with the Federal Government*
Superintendent of Documents
Government Printing Office
Washington, DC 20402

*Federal Acquisition Regulations*
Superintendent of Documents
Government Printing Office
Washington, DC 20402

Federal Procurement Data Center
4040 North Fairfax Drive, Ste. 900
Arlington, VA 22003

*Federal Procurement Update*
P.O. Box 90608
Washington, DC 20090
(Monthly publication providing insight into federal procurement regulations and policies)

*Government Contracts Reports*
Commerce Clearing House Inc.
4025 West Peterson Avenue
Chicago, IL 60646
(Weekly publication)

Government Data Publications
1661 McDonald Avenue
Brooklyn, NY 11230
(Publishes monthly and annual directories of contract leads and awards)

*Guide to the Preparation of Offers for Selling to the Military*
Superintendent of Documents
U.S. Government Printing Office
Washington, DC 20402

*Guide to Government Contracting*
Commerce Clearing House Inc.
4025 West Peterson Avenue
Chicago, IL 60646
(Monthly publication)

*How to Prepare Bids*
Contact your local regional office of the Small Business Administration

*Procurement Automated Support System (PASS)*
U.S. Small Business Administration
P.O. Box 9000
Melbourne, FL 32902-9919

*Selling to the Military*
Superintendent of Documents
U.S. Government Printing Office
Washington, DC 20402

*Small Business Specialists*
Superintendent of Documents
U.S. Government Printing Office
Washington, DC 20402

*Small Business Subcontracting Directory*
Superintendent of Documents
U.S. Government Printing Office
Washington, DC 20402

*U.S. Government Purchasing and Sales Directory*
Superintendent of Documents
U.S. Government Printing Office
Washington, DC 20402

*Women Business Owner: Selling to the Federal Government*
Superintendent of Documents
U.S. Government Printing Office
Washington, DC 20402

**Specifications, Commercial:**
American National Standards Institute
1430 Broadway
New York, NY 10018

Global Engineering Documents
2805 McCaw Avenue
P.O. Box 19539
Irvine, CA 92713-9539

Society of Automotive Engineers
400 Commonwealth Drive
Warrendale, PA 15096-0001

**Specifications, Federal:**
Specifications Unit
7th and D Streets, SW
Washington, DC 20407

**Specifications, Military:**
Commanding Officer
Naval Publications and Forms Center
5701 Tabor Avenue
Philadelphia, PA 19120

## Other Sources of Information

### Small Business Administration Regional Offices

*Region 1: Maine, New Hampshire, Vermont, Massachusetts, Rhode Island, and Connecticut*

Small Business Administration
60 Batterymarch, 10th Floor
Boston, MA 02110

*Region 2: New York, New Jersey, Puerto Rico, Virgin Islands*

Small Business Administration
26 Federal Plaza, Room 29-118
New York, NY 10278

*Region 3: Pennsylvania, Delaware, Maryland, Virginia, West Virginia, and Washington, DC*

Small Business Administration
475 Allendale Road, Suite 201
King of Prussia, PA 19406

*Region 4: North Carolina, South Carolina, Georgia, Florida, Mississippi, Alabama, Tennessee, and Kentucky*

Small Business Administration
1375 Peachtree Street, NE
Atlanta, GA 30367

*Region 5: Ohio, Indiana, Michigan, Illinois, Wisconsin, and Minnesota*

Small Business Administration
230 South Dearborn Street, Room 510
Chicago, IL 60604

*Region 6: Louisiana, Arkansas, Texas, Oklahoma, and New Mexico*

Small Business Administration
8635 King George Drive, Bldg. C
Dallas, TX 75235-3391

*Region 7: Missouri, Kansas, Iowa, and Nebraska*

Small Business Administration
911 Walnut Street, 13th Floor
Kansas City, MO 64106

*Region 8: North Dakota, South Dakota, Colorado, Wyoming, Utah, and Montana*

Small Business Administration
999 18th Street Ste. 701
Denver, CO 80202-2395

*Region 9: California, Arizona, Nevada, Hawaii, Guam, Trust Territories, and American Samoa*

Small Business Administration
450 Golden Gate Avenue, Box 36044
San Francisco, CA 94102

*Region 10: Oregon, Washington, Idaho, and Alaska*

Small Business Administration
2615 4th Avenue, Room 400
Seattle, WA 98121

## Reference Books

*Standard Industrial Classification Manual*
National Technical Information Service
5285 Port Royal Road
Springfield, VA 22161
(Explains SIC codes)

*Wards Business Directory*
Information Access Company, a division of
Zeff-Davis Publishing Company
11 Davis Drive
Belmont, CA 94002
(Provides business contact lists)

Holtz, Herman, and Terry Schmidt
*The Winning Proposal, How to Write It*
McGraw-Hill (1981)

Kerzner, H.
*Project Management: A Systems Approach to Planning, Scheduling, and Controlling*
Van Nostrand Reinhold (1979)
(Provides guidance for program management)

Koontz, H., and C. O'Donnell
*Management: A Systems and Contingency Analysis of Managerial Functions*
McGraw-Hill (1976)

McVay, Barry L.
*Proposals That Win Federal Contracts*
Panoptic Enterprises (1989)
(Provides guidance for writing proposals)

## Project Management Software

Instaplan Corporation
655 Redwood Highway, Suite 311
Mill Valley, CA 94941

Microsoft Project
One Microsoft Way
Redmond, WA 98052

Time Line
Symantec Corporation
7200 Redwood Boulevard
Novato, CA 94945

# Glossary

**Acquisition:** The procurement by contract, using appropriated funds, of supplies or services for the use of the federal government through purchase or lease.

**Administrative contracting officer (ACO):** A government representative whose job it is to administer contracts. Usually assigned by the contracting officer.

**Amendment (of solicitation):** A document used to make changes to a solicitation after it is issued but before the deadline for receiving proposals.

**Basic Ordering Agreement (BOA):** A written, although unofficial, agreement of understanding of the supplies or services to be provided by a contractor.

**Best and Final Offer (BAFO):** An offer requested by the government after original offer has been submitted and reviewed. Often used as a tool for negotiation.

**Bid Opening Date (BOD):** The date on which bids for a particular solicitation will be opened and evaluated by the government.

**Certificate of Competency (COC):** A document issued by the Small Business Administration certifying a small firm's ability to carry out a federal contract.

**Code of Federal Regulations (CFR):** A set of rules, divided into 50 titles, published by the various executive departments and agencies of the federal government.

***Commerce Business Daily* (CBD):** The daily newspaper published by the U.S. Government Printing Office that summarizes bidding opportunities on government contracts valued at more than $25,000. It also describes recent awards, provides leads on subcontracting opportunities, outlines foreign business opportunities, and provides information about seminars and other events of interest to government contractors.

**Commercial Item Description (CID):** A document describing the physical and performance characteristics of a commercially available product.

**Contract Administration Office:** A government office that handles various functions related to the administration of contracts.

**Contract Data Requirements List (CDRL):** A document used to order an item contained in a solicitation.

**Contract Line Item Number (CLIN):** A number assigned to identify each item purchased in a contract.

**Contracting Office:** A government office that awards and executes a contract for products or services.

**Contracting Officer:** A government representative whose job it is to enter, administrate, or terminate contracts. The official responsible for making sure the contract is properly performed and conforms to the rules.

**Data Item Description (DID):** A document that describes the specific requirements for preparing a data item that is part of a solicitation.

**Data Universal Numbering System (DUNS):** The number assigned to each government contractor's plant or location, as required by the FAR.

**Debriefing:** A meeting conducted by the government to provide unsuccessful offerors with a basis for the selection decision and contract award.

**Defense Acquisition Regulations (DAR):** Also called DFAR for Defense Federal Acquisition Regulations. Procurement regulations used as a supplement to the Federal Acquisition Regulations.

**Department of Defense (DOD) Form 558-1:** The Form companies fill out to be listed as approved Department of Defense bidders.

**Destination inspection:** A requirement for the government to inspect a product at the place where it is received.

**Disadvantaged business:** A business which is at least 51 percent owned by one or more socially and economically disadvantaged individuals and is managed on a daily basis by one or more such persons.

**8(a) Business:** A business at least 51 percent owned by a person or persons who is determined to be socially and economically disadvantaged under the guidelines of Section 8(a) of the Small Business Act of 1953.

**Federal Acquisition Regulation (FAR):** The government's procurement rules. Part of the Code of Federal Regulations.

**Federal Procurement Data Center (FPDC):** Clearinghouse of data on what federal agencies are buying.

**Federal Supply Code (FSC):** Numbering system used to categorize federal suppliers by their specific product.

**General Services Administration (GSA):** Umbrella government purchasing agency that buys many commonly used products and services for other agencies.

**General Services Board of Contract Appeals (GSBCA):** Acts as a reviewer of protests on contract awards when petitioned.

**Government Accounting Office (GAO):** Agency responsible for government accounting policy. Acts as a reviewer of protests on contract awards when petitioned.

**Government Printing Office (GPO):** The publisher of the *Commerce Business Daily* and other contracting forms and publications. Also, a major purchaser of many kinds of goods and services related to printing and publishing.

**Guidance conference:** Meeting held by the government to give a contractor instructions on a specific requirement of a contract.

**IAW (in accordance with):** Used in contracts to refer to regulations, specifications, or other requirements with which a product or service will have to conform.

**Invitation for Bid (IFB):** A government solicitation or request sent out to prospective bidders. It describes exactly what the government wants and asks for offers based on those specifications.

**Last and Final Offer (LAFO):** Offer requested by the government after original offer has been submitted and reviewed. Often used as a tool for negotiation.

**Military Specification (Mil-Spec):** An exact description of goods or services purchased by the Department of Defense, Army, Navy or other military agency.

**Military Standard (Mil-Std):** A Department of Defense document that describes technical or engineering limitations to which a product or service has to perform.

**National Stock Number (NSN):** A unique catalog number assigned by the General Services Administration organizing items by groups and classes.

**Negotiation:** Contracting through the use of proposals and discussions rather than through specifications and bids.

**Offer:** A response to a solicitation that, if accepted, binds the offeror to perform the contract. Responses to invitations for bids (sealed bidding) are called *bids or* sealed bids. Responses to requests for proposals (negotiation) are called *proposals*. Responses to requests for quotations (negotiation) are not offers and are called *quotes*.

**Offeror:** Generally, a bidder on a government contract.

**Point of contact (POC):** The contracting officer or other government employee designated as the person bidders are to contact with questions.

**Postaward conference:** A meeting conducted by the government to orient the contractor on the requirements of a new contract.

**Preaward survey:** A meeting held by the government to determine a contractor's capabilities to perform if awarded a contract.

**Preinvitation Notice (PIN):** A short summary of a solicitation which is sent to prospective bidders. Interested bidders can then ask to see the whole solicitation packages.

**Preproposal conference:** A meeting held by the government to allow interested parties to ask questions about a solicitation, prior to submitting a proposal. Sometimes referred to as a bidder's conference.

**Prime contractor, or prime:** A person or business that has entered into a contract with the government.

**Procurement:** A government purchase.

**Procurement Automated Source System (PASS):** A central, computerized inventory system for matching small businesses up with contracting or subcontracting opportunities.

**Progress payments:** Method by which the government pays a contractor as work progresses. Payments may be as frequent as monthly.

**Protest:** A written objection by an interested party to a particular solicitation or to the proposed award of a contract.

**Request for Information (RFI):** A sort of preliminary request for proposal, in which the government requests potential bidders to submit ideas, concepts, and information about how they would fulfill the potential contract.

**Request for Proposal (RFP):** A solicitation describing generally what the government wants and how bids will be evaluated. It is not as specific as an Invitation for Bid, may allow for negotiation, and may award a contract based on a combination of price and technical merit.

**Request for Quote (RFQ):** An informational document, not a solicitation, that the government issues when seeking price, delivery, or other information that will help it in planning.

**Section 8(a):** Part of the Small Business Act of 1953 aimed at helping disadvantaged-owned small firms land government contracts.

**Small business:** A business which is independently owned and operated, is not dominant in the field for which it is competing for government contracts, and also qualifies as to number of employees, average annual sales, or other criteria set by the Small Business Administration. The Code of Federal Regulations, Title 13, Part 121, contains detailed industry definitions and specifications.

**Small Business Administration (SBA):** Federal agency set up by the Small Business Act of 1953 and charged with seeing small businesses get a fair share of federal procurements.

**Small business liaison officer (SBLO):** An employee of a major prime contractor who is assigned to administer small business subcontracts.

**Small business set-aside (SBSA):** A bid opportunity that is restricted to small business bidders.

**Sole source:** A business picked by the government as the only qualified supplier of a good or service.

**Solicitation:** A document such as an Invitation For Bid, Request for Quote, or Request For Proposal that describes what the government wants to buy.

**Solicitation mailing list:** A list maintained by the contracting office of all eligible companies that have sent in solicitation mailing list applications or are deemed able to meet the requirements of a contract by the contracting office.

**Source inspection:** A requirement for the government to inspect a product at the source of manufacture.

**Standard Form (SF) 129:** Form to fill out to get on civilian agency solicitation mailing lists.

**Standard Industrial Classification (SIC):** A code used to categorize manufacturers by their specialty.

**Statement of Work (SOW):** A document written by a buying agency to define the specific efforts required to perform a task that is part of a solicitation.

**Subcontractor:** A business that has entered into a contract with a prime contractor.

**Uniform Contract Format (UCF):** The required method of structuring a solicitation as detailed in the Code of Federal Regulations. The UCF divides the solicitation into four parts and 16 sections.

**Unsolicited proposal:** A written proposal that is submitted to an agency solely on the initiative of the submitter, not in response to a request by the government.

**Women-owned business:** A business that is at least 51 percent owned by a woman or women who are U.S. citizens and who also control and operate the business.

# Index

## About the Authors

CLINTON L. CROWNOVER is president of Crownover Communications, Independence, Missouri, a consulting firm specializing in proposal writing, logistics support, and other technical services. He has more than a decade of experience in procuring government contracts.

MARK HENRICKS is a New York City writer and editor specializing in small business. His articles have appeared in publications such as *The New York Times, Working Woman, PC World,* and *Small Business Reports*. Mr. Henricks also writes a monthly column for *Entrepreneur* magazine.